Clay Shooting for Beginners and Enthusiasts

John King

Clay Shooting for Beginners and Enthusiasts

John King

Copyright © John King 2009

The text pages of this book are produced via an independent certification process that ensures the trees from which the paper is produced come from well-managed sources that exclude the risk of using illegally logged timber and/or are printed on recycled paper. A supplemental **DVD** ISBN 978-09563461-2-4 can be purchased from all the major book retailers in the United Kingdom or previewed and purchased at www.johnkingcoaching.com

ISBN: 978-0-9563461-1-7

Published by John King Coaching

www.johnkingcoaching.com

admin@johnkingcoaching.com

Printed and bound by www.printondemand-worldwide.com

Titles By John King

Books & eBooks

Clay Shooting For Beginners and Enthusiasts (Print edition ISBN 9780956346117)
Clay Shooting For Beginners and Enthusiasts (Kindle edition 9780956346131)
Clay Shooting For Beginners and Enthusiasts (iBooks edition ISBN 9780956346155)
Game Shooting (Print edition ISBN 9780992629205)
Game Shooting (Kindle edition ISBN 9780992629212)
Game Shooting (iBooks edition 9780992629229)

DVDs

Clay Shooting From Scratch DVD (ISBN 9780956346124)
Sporting Clays Shooting From Scratch NTSC version For USA TV systems
(ISBN 9780956346186)

John King's eBooks can be purchased from Amazon's Kindle Store and Apple's iBookstore. In the United Kingdom Books and DVDs can be purchased form all the major book retailers, or previewed and purchased at:

www.johnkingcoaching.com

This book is dedicated to

Maureen

Acknowledgements

Special thanks to James and Caroline, whose enthusiasm instigated this re-write, and whose team turned my scribbled sketches into actual diagrams.

To Richard for his camera skills and his abundance of invaluable generous input from his vast source of knowledge of clay shooting.

To James 'O' and Andy 'B' who so patiently applied their computing skills to make order from my jumbled mass of ideas, words, diagrams and pictures.

Finally of course to Louise my model pupil.

Contents

Foreword

More years ago than either of us care to remember, I was lucky enough to start clay target shooting under the watchful gaze of John King.

Like so many others before me, I became totally consumed by the sport and made rapid progress up the rankings, eventually taking a career diversion into shooting journalism.

I have been lucky, as a result, to work with many of the top competitors and coaches in the world but, for all that I have done since then, my shooting has been built on the foundations that John gave me and the simple, repeatable techniques he teaches.

He has that enviable knack of saying little yet communicating a lot and there are literally hundreds of keen shooters who are safer, better shots as the result.

This revision to his book is long overdue. There is plenty of advice available for those already hooked on the sport and looking to go further, but little that cuts so effectively through the jargon and the mystery for the newcomer. This new edition fills that gap and will hopefully inspire many more to experience the thrill of breaking clays.

Richard Rawlingson
Editor - Clay Shooting magazine (1994-2006)

Introduction

This book is intended to encourage those of you who have been thinking of taking up shooting to 'have a go'! I hope it will also reassure you that there is a logical and relatively simple route to safe, competent and pleasurable shooting. The book is also aimed at those of you who have recently begun shooting; to help with sorting out the mass of bewildering information that you might have picked up from your shooting friends.

If you are already an experienced shooter, you may be disappointed that there is very little technical information here, but I would like to think that you can combine this simple set of guidelines with your accumulated experience to improve your shooting. It should also provide you with a systematic guide to passing on your shooting skills and pleasures to new enthusiasts.

This simple approach is certainly not intended to patronise or insult the intelligence of the reader. It is my experience that adults attending the shooting school are 'intelligent achievers' who are inclined to attach too much intellect to the learning process. Subconsciously, they continually attempt to complicate something that is a relatively simple process. I have chosen it deliberately, as the subjects covered are those that I find beginners need, and wish to know about.

I also find that once pupils have reached their own satisfactory standard of shooting, they tend to follow their individual interest within one or more of the clay or field disciplines, where they then seek further knowledge from the great variety of specialist shooting publications, videos and DVDs.

How this book works

This book follows a typical course of shooting school lessons taken by someone who has never previously fired a shotgun.

The lessons and discussions represent the logical course of events undertaken by many beginner pupils at the shooting school.

Throughout the book I will be writing as if I were speaking with you at the school; you should find that using this book to practice in your head helps enormously when used in parallel with a practical course.

During the first lesson you are taught safety, the basic parts and operation of a shotgun, and how to kill a simple single crossing and single driven target. You will shoot a single crossing clay moving right to left, and then a single driven clay coming straight towards you, passing overhead.

The second and subsequent lessons include double targets (two clays). The third lesson introduces gun mounting (bringing the gun stock correctly to the cheek and shoulder).

The lessons then progress onto more difficult clay targets sufficient to provide the novice pupil with the technique and confidence to tackle typical sporting clay shooting combinations including 'doubles'.

Initial instruction is given on typical sporting clay targets only. However, most novice pupils quickly add to their shooting pleasure by reading shooting publications, and naturally ask me for explanations of other clay shooting disciplines. Therefore a chapter is set aside to describe the basics of the great variety of types of clay shooting.

Questions and myths surrounding clay target shooting

Before beginning the first shooting lesson, I would like to give some general answers to recurring questions asked by people who are thinking of taking up shooting, and hopefully dispel some common doubts and fears.

The most common fear that I encounter is that shooting a shotgun has to be a physically painful process: This is definitely not necessary, though sadly this continues to be the unfortunate experience for many people. They suffer pain and discomfort because they are encouraged to 'have a go' using the wrong gun with the wrong cartridge, and are not given proper guidance and assistance.

I can answer the common question of "where do I go to have a try at shooting?" by telling you how to ensure that you do not suffer pain when you shoot for the first time: Go to a reputable shooting school and be taught by a professional coach. The coach will ensure that you use a shotgun suitable to your physical stature, ie one that you can hold comfortably and which fires a cartridge that does not cause a recoil which will hurt you. You will also be shown and helped to hold the gun properly and safely before you are allowed to fire it.

A reputable shooting school will also provide you with earmuffs and shooting safety glasses.

I regularly hear comments such as, "I have always wanted to try clay target shooting, but I do not think I would be able to do it". There seems to be a common idea that shotgun shooting requires some super physical attributes and particular mental abilities. None of this is true!

The simple honest answer to the question of "who can shoot?" is "anyone who wants to"! I learned many years ago that adults who arrive at the shooting school for a first lesson possess every conceivable mental and physical attribute to be a successful shot.

The logic is very simple: What person of normal intelligence takes the trouble to find a shooting school, then allocate the time and expense, if they do not truly believe that they will achieve success?

How successful they are depends entirely on three factors: Time, budget, and - most importantly - motivation - i.e. how good the individual wants to be. My task is simple: I merely have to feed each person's visual, auditory and kinaesthetic senses (seeing, hearing and feeling). I just provide words, pictures and doing experiences which, to my constant joy, ensures that everyone succeeds.

Age at either end of the scale is immaterial. The deciding factor is that the pupil is of sufficient physical stature to hold and shoot a suitable gun without suffering discomfort. He or she must have sufficient mental abilities to understand and follow simple instructions and be able to see a moving disc about the size of a saucer up to about 50 yards away - even wearing glasses is not a barrier. The most important attribute is the desire to learn. In recent months I have given tuition to pupils from 8 to 80 years old.

The 'anyone who wants to' range certainly includes the disabled. There is no reason why someone in a wheelchair cannot enjoy shooting. If they are capable of holding and pointing a shotgun, they will be successful.

At long last the mythical idea that shotgun shooting is a 'men only' activity is also rapidly changing. There never have been any valid reasons why ladies cannot enjoy shooting as much as men. It has been historical social attitudes only that have prevented many ladies from enjoying the sport.

Many of my female pupils are of the most petite and feminine stature. They are able to shoot completely without discomfort and as competently as anyone else.

The excitement of clay target shooting

The attraction of shooting as an outdoor activity is obvious. It can be enjoyed at any level; if you choose to use it as an occasional leisure pursuit and are happy to kill 10 out of 30 clays, you will have just as much pleasure as the competitive clay

shooter who shoots at every available opportunity and shoots mainly to better the scores of others.

You can only fully understand that special excitement of killing your first clay and that particular satisfaction of improving your personal score by trying it.

Come and try it with me!

Lesson One
Equipment and 'The Method'

Welcome to your first shooting lesson. During this session I am going to show you the kit you will be using, and teach you how to kill moving clay targets using the simple sequences of the Method.

The Method is a minimum sequence of co-ordinated eye, brain, hand and body movements that let you learn the basics of successful shotgun shooting very quickly. This simple approach to teaching shooting was devised by the Clay Pigeon Shooting Association's tutorial staff. Its effectiveness lies in its total simplicity: As a right handed person, the Method encourages you to use the shotgun as though you are merely pointing with your left hand (reverse for left handers).

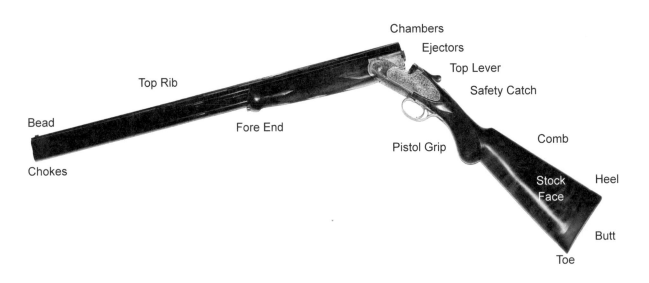

Follow my instructions on the simple movements of the Method and you will be successfully killing clay targets in a very short while.

Introducing a shot gun

The gun that you are going to shoot during this lesson is a single trigger over and under 28 bore. Note it is open and empty! The over and under simply describes one barrel being set on top of the other. The gun is capable of firing two cartridges by a first then second squeeze of the trigger, although you will only be firing singles during your first lesson.

I have chosen this particular gun as I am sure that you will be able to hold and shoot it comfortably. Pupils attending for their first lesson are often concerned about being hurt by the recoil of the gun. This one is ideal for ladies and youngsters shooting for the first time; its light weight makes it easy to hold plus it has very little recoil.

You do not need any technical knowledge of guns to shoot successfully, but you should of course know the basic parts and how to open, close and fire the gun safely.

Starting from the open end of the barrels is a small pip called the bead. It is not a sight, but merely a reference point: Treat it just the same as the end of your index finger, as you would when pointing.

The first two to three inches of the barrels immediately under the bead are the "chokes" (constricted to varying degrees) to tighten or open the pattern of the shotgun pellets. This gun has the chokes opened right out and therefore throws a wide pattern of pellets to give you the greatest chance of killing the clay targets.

The flat strip of metal along the top of the barrels is called the rib and is designed to lead your eye naturally in the direction of the target that you are shooting. This piece of wood that wraps around the barrels is the forend; it will afford a comfortable grip for your left hand, whilst also protecting your hand from the heat of the barrels.

Immediately behind the forend is the breech and action that contains the firing mechanisms of the gun. The ends of the barrels that fit into the action are called the chambers.

The pieces of metal at the sides of the chambers are the extractors which eject the fired cartridges when the gun has been opened after firing. The gun is opened by pushing a lever on top of the action to the right. Immediately behind the top lever is the combined safety catch and barrel selector. Sliding the selector to the right or left dictates whether the top or bottom barrel fires first. When the safety catch is slid to the rear, the trigger mechanism cannot fire the gun, though it is most important to understand that the safety catch to the 'on' position only prevents the gun being fired by pulling the trigger! A hard jolt or knock to the gun could cause it to fire. **Shotguns are only safe when open and empty!** The wood behind the safety catch is called the grip. In this case, it is a pistol grip which allows your right hand to wrap around it tightly whilst your right fore finger slides naturally into the trigger guard and onto the trigger. Leading back from the grip is the stock. The top part of the stock is the comb, and at the very end of the stock is the butt.

Handling a shot gun safely

Now I will show you the safe and acceptable ways to hold and handle a shotgun. When you are attending clay shoots it is most important that you are seen to handle the gun correctly. **The golden rule is always to treat a closed shotgun as though it is loaded.**

Firstly, how to take a shotgun from its gun slip (bag). Even when the gun is in its slip, you can see which is the barrel end. Hold the slip so that the barrels are pointed towards the ground, undo the slip, slide the right hand onto the grip of the gun, making sure that the fingers do not go into the trigger guard. Pull the gun from the slip, and - as the barrels come into view - open the gun with the thumb on the top lever.

Taking a closed gun from a gun rack is a similar operation, except the gun is in full view and standing with the barrels pointing upwards. Remember you are treating the closed gun as though it is loaded! Grip the forend firmly with your left hand, taking care not to place any part of your body over the choke end of the barrels. Lift the gun from the rack and turn it so that the barrels point towards the ground, making sure that the barrels do not point at anyone! Hold the grip firmly with the right hand keeping your index finger out of the trigger guard. Place the action and stock of the gun against the hip and open the gun.

Always carry out these movements when taking any shotgun from a slip or rack.

Open the gun as you remove it from the slip

Now I will show you four safe, acceptable ways to hold and carry an empty shotgun when clay shooting. One of the most comfortable is with the choked end of the barrels resting on the right foot. The right hand holds the grip with the right fore finger placed along the side of the action. Now the weight of the gun is supported by the foot and rests comfortably alongside the right leg and hip. The barrels will not be damaged or fouled by anything on the ground.

You can also stand or walk comfortably with the open gun carried over the right forearm, as the gun will have additional support from the side of your body and your upper arm.

An open empty shotgun: Resting the barrels on the foot ensures they don't become fouled by anything on the ground

21

An open shotgun: Resting safely and comfortably over the arm

An open shotgun: Resting safely and comfortably over the shoulder

A third safe and comfortable way to walk with an open gun is to rest the action on the right shoulder with the barrels pointing downwards and forward. The right hand wraps firmly around the barrels just below the forend; the gun is now held securely in place with its weight supported by the shoulder.

I suggest you choose just one of these three, however all are correct as everyone in your vicinity can readily see that the gun is open and empty.

The fourth way of carrying your empty gun is conveniently in its slip. Placing the shoulder strap over the right shoulder allows the body to support the weight of the gun whilst leaving the hands free to carry cartridges etc. The gun will also be protected by the slip from damage.

An empty shotgun: Carried safely and comfortably in a gun slip whenever possible

Essential head-gear

I have shown you how to carry the gun safely and comfortably; now I am going to provide you with three pieces of equipment for your comfort and safety.

I would like you to wear a hat like this during the lesson, and suggest you adopt the habit of wearing a hat whenever you are shooting. You will soon learn that complete comfort is essential for successful shooting. This hat has a large peak, although any hat which has a peak or brim and is comfortable will suffice. A hat will keep your head warm and dry in inclement weather, while the brim or peak will help shield your eyes from the sun and rain, and will reduce unnecessary peripheral vision, helping you to focus better on the moving target. The peak of the hat will also be important for protecting your head, face and eyes from broken pieces of clay falling from the sky.

Earmuffs will add to your comfort by reducing the noise of the cartridge being fired. Crucially, it will protect your ears from being damaged by the shock wave produced by each fired cartridge. Be in no doubt that regular shotgun shooting will cause damage to your hearing if you do not protect your ears by always wearing earmuffs.

Thirdly, these shooting safety glasses will protect your eyes from fragments of clay target, and the ultra violet lenses will also improve your vision.

It is also just as important to protect your ears and eyes when you are in proximity to other people who are shooting.

The dangerous power of a shot gun

Before I explain the safety rules when actually shooting the gun, I am going to demonstrate the effect of a shotgun fired at close range. Once seen it is never forgotten. I do not do it to frighten you. I do it because I strongly believe that anyone who is going to handle a loaded shotgun should understand that they are in control of a piece of equipment that is designed to **kill** and will do so most effectively.

When people are killed or maimed with a shot fired from a shotgun, it is invariably at close range. It is **never** an accident: Someone has either been criminally deliberate, or stupidly negligent!

Let's have a look. Put your earmuffs and glasses on and adjust them to fit comfortably. Now focus on the mark I have put on a piece of corrugated iron in front of us. Note the ends of the barrels are about two yards from it. I will load one cartridge and shoot at that mark.

Horrific, isn't it? That hole about the size of my fist was caused by a mass of lead made up of little pellets. At this close range the pellets have not travelled sufficient distance to open up into a spread pattern. That mass of lead struck the sheet of iron travelling at about 1,400 feet per second!

Keep your earmuffs and glasses on and I will fire one more cartridge to demonstrate the spread of the pattern at 20 yards, which is the sort of distance you will be killing clays at.

I am going to shoot at the centre of that white painted metal plate (see overleaf) and then let you have a look at the pattern. There, now you can see all the tiny

Artist's impression of a clay target caught in a string of shot

The hole made by a light load (23g) cartridge fired from an open choked 20 bore gun

marks where the pellets struck the plate, and that the pellets have spread out into an irregular circle about 30" in diameter.

This plate only shows the landing pattern or spread pattern of the shot, however in reality the pellets travel through the air as a 'string' of shot. Something like a large cigar or sausage with ragged edges about 10 feet long.

The single right-to-left crossing clay target

Now I will show you the clay you are going to kill (see overleaf). Close up you can see it is a small black disc looking a bit like a thick edged saucer upside down. This clay target is made of a mixture of

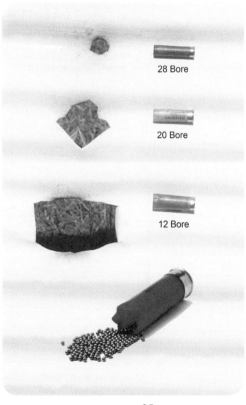

28 Bore

20 Bore

12 Bore

The shot pattern from an Open Choked (true cylinder) 20 Bore

The shot pattern from a Choked (3/4) 12 Bore

A standard sized clay held up against a tight shot pattern

26

pitch and lime. It is strong enough to remain intact as it is thrown from the clay target trap, but quite brittle and easily broken when struck by a few shotgun pellets. These clays are totally biodegradable, so the broken pieces soon rot away to a harmless dust.

Now look at a few clays in flight, one at a time. This is a single crossing target. The clay will appear about 70 yards in front of you, slightly to your right. It will fly towards you, crossing from right to left, and passing in front and above you at about 20 – 25 yards. That target is the first one you are going to kill, using the sequences of the Method.

'The Method'

Before you can shoot the Method you must decide upon your 'kill point' and 'pick up' point. First choose the kill point; this is a position somewhere along the flight path of the target where you have most chance of killing it. It is mainly a matter of timing: Try to kill it too soon and you will end up rushing your shot. Wait too long and you probably will have twisted your body to an awkward position and will be trying to kill a clay that is dropping from its smooth regular flight path.

Point to a position on this clay's flight path that you have chosen as your kill point. I suggest that you move your kill point a little further to your left. Good, that is ideal. Now point at your chosen pick up point. Well, you're pointing straight at the position where the clay is thrown from the trap. It is travelling fastest there, so move your pick up point a little distance to the left. There, you will now see the clay much better against a clear sky background.

Remember that I told you earlier that the Method was a systematic way of learning to point a shotgun naturally. If you were merely pointing at a moving object you would use your feet to turn your body to face the object you were pointing at.

So, having chosen your kill point, set your feet so your body faces towards that spot. Whenever you are shooting, always imagine that you are stood within a

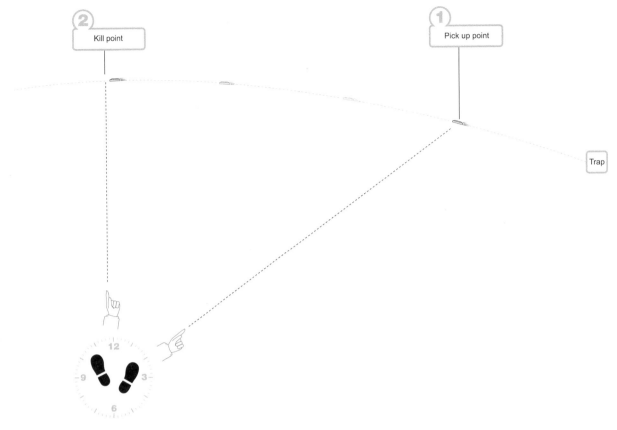

Feet position, pick up point and kill point for a Single right to left Crossing target

clock face, and that your kill point is always 12 o'clock. Place your feet at about five-past-eleven, and stand comfortably with your heels about 6 – 8 inches apart.

Always carry out this 'kill point/clock face' check to ensure that your feet will turn your body naturally towards the point where you are going to fire the gun. If you do not check your feet position you will find that you have instinctively faced the position where the target first appears.

The next stage is to get you to point at the target in flight. Put your feet in the five-past-eleven position and point at your chosen kill point with your left fore finger. Keep your left arm slightly bent and relaxed. Now move your arm back along the target's expected flight path to your chosen pick up point. Call 'pull' and point at the clay in flight with your left hand, keeping both eyes open.

Good, just repeat that a few times. Each time you point at the clay it seems a little easier and you begin to feel you have more time.

You have already learned the basis of the Method. There are only two more stages which I am going to teach you by getting you to point the unloaded gun at the clay in flight. But first, you must know how to hold and point the gun comfortably.

A correct gun mount

You can see that the gun is empty, so I will close it and show you how it fits into the shoulder. My right hand is holding the grip firmly and my right forefinger is placed alongside the action. The butt is bedded firmly into my shoulder pocket, with the comb pressed into the soft part of my cheek. The gun is now held securely by the combined three point lock of: Right hand, cheek and shoulder pocket.

Now the left hand hold. The left hand holds the forend loosely with the left fore finger pointing forward along the side. Pointing the finger prevents me from gripping the forend too tightly, which would tense my arm muscles and prevent me from pointing naturally.

Gun locked very tightly into the cheek and shoulder

29

Correct left hand hold

The pointing finger is also a psychological reminder that the barrels of the gun are merely an extension of the left hand, and that they are simply being pointed at a moving target.

Holding the gun in this way ensures that the head and eyes stay in line with the barrels, and that the body absorbs the recoil without discomfort.

Now you take the empty gun and stand at the firing point with your feet set up as I showed you earlier. To close the gun, hold it against your hip with the right hand. Ensure that the gun is angled downwards, then hold the barrels by the forend and push them away from you firmly. The stock, action and your body are now being used as a simple effective lever to close the gun comfortably and safely.

Keep your right forefinger out of the trigger guard by placing it alongside the action. Now mount the gun into your shoulder. Relax your grip with the right hand while I move the stock so that the butt is bedded into the shoulder pocket. Tighten your right hand hold and pull the stock back into your shoulder and the comb into the soft part of your cheek.

Loosen your left hand hold and move it back towards you a little bit. Now your left arm is more natural and relaxed.

The unfamiliar weight of the gun will tend to force you backwards. Lean forward into the gun, so that most of your weight is over your left foot. Now your left foot will act as a natural pivot point on which to turn the top half of your body as you point the gun at the moving target.

Now practice bringing the gun down from your shoulder, opening and closing it, then putting it back into the mounted position. Do this a few times. Remember to angle the whole gun downwards before you open it, so the barrels are still pointing safely at the ground as you close them against the action.

Back to the Method. Remember the barrels of the gun are an extension of your left hand which you are going to point at a moving target. You will be pointing correctly when you see the clay sat just above the bead at the end of the barrels.

From now on, whenever I ask you to point at a clay target I am in reality asking you to sit the barrels underneath it. You must see a little daylight between the clay and the bead.

Shotguns are set up to place about two thirds of the pattern above where the gun is pointing. This is to allow the shooter to keep a good, clear view of the target and to ensure that it is caught in the centre of the pattern.

Mount the gun comfortably into the shoulder, point the barrels at the kill point, then wind them back along the clay's expected flight path to the pick up point. Call 'pull' and simply point at the clay in flight. Sit the clay just above the bead.

Now for the last two movements of the Method. If you fire the gun whilst you are pointing directly at the moving target (which is what your brain will want to do), the pattern of shot will miss it behind.

Whilst your eyes and brain are sending messages to your trigger finger to 'squeeze' and whilst the shot is taking time to travel through the air, the target is still moving!

To allow for this 'delay time' the barrels must be moved ahead of the target in order that the pattern of shot will strike and 'kill' it. In your minds eye you should see the barrels leading the target. This distance should be seen as the 'lead picture', also called a 'kill picture'. It varies, of course, depending on speed, distance and angle of the moving target in relation to the shooter. I will show you the appropriate lead picture for this target.

Can you see the distance between the end of the barrels and this clay I'm holding up to the right of them? This is the lead picture you must see to kill this target. The size of the gap between clay and barrel is the picture you make in relation to the target in the air.

The Lead Picture (or Kill Picture) that you need to create for this right to left crossing target

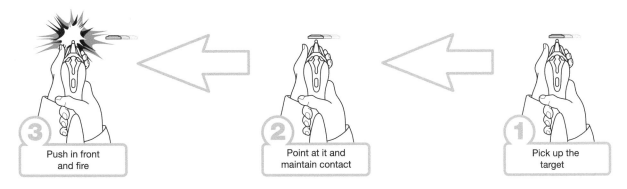

3 Push in front and fire

2 Point at it and maintain contact

1 Pick up the target

The Method applied to a right to left crossing target

Having pointed at the target from the pick up point, you should establish the lead picture just before it has reached the kill point. You do this by making a controlled acceleration of your left hand. I call this controlled acceleration the 'push', so whenever I say "push", make your lead picture and squeeze the trigger.

That might all seem a lot to remember so let me summarise: **Pick up the target (point at it), move the barrels with the clay, push the barrels in front of the clay (make the lead picture) and fire.**

Now you can practice the whole Method, but the gun will only be loaded with a snap cap – that's a dummy cartridge which allows you to squeeze the trigger and activate the firing pin without causing strain to the firing mechanism.

The whole sequence will be: Feet in the correct position; mount the gun; point the barrels at the kill point; wind barrels back to the pick up point; finger alongside the trigger; call "pull"; pick up the target; point at it; move with it; push the barrels in front of the target (make the lead picture); and fire. Bring the gun down and open it.

As you open the gun, the snap cap will eject as a spent cartridge would. I will reload the snap caps for you. Ready? Call "pull", point at the clay, push in front, fire. Gun down and open. Good. Repeat that a few times. You are doing well and are carrying out the correct movements of the Method.

33

However, there is one minor problem. As you point the barrels at the clay, I notice that you are always pointing to the left – or slightly in front of it. I suspect your left eye is stronger than your right. In shooting terms, you have a left 'Master Eye'.

I would like you to repeat the Method movements again but this time, close your left eye as you pick up the target.

Ready? Call "pull", point at it, move with it, push in front. That is better. Now you are actually pointing the gun straight at the target until you make your lead picture. Don't worry about having the 'wrong' Master Eye, it is very common and does not mean that there is anything wrong with your eyesight.

I will show you the effects of a wrong 'master eye' on the pattern plate at the end of this lesson.

The safety rules

Next, the safety rules that you **must** adhere to when you are actually shooting.

• You must only point a loaded gun at the designated clay target. You must never point it at any person or living thing. If you are distracted by any noise or movement you must immediately bring the gun to the down position and open it.

• If the clay appears broken, or flies at a different angle from its expected flight path, or appears before you are ready, bring the gun down and open it.

• As soon as you have fired the gun, bring it down and open it.

• Most important of all: If ever you squeeze the trigger when the gun is loaded and the gun does not fire; bring it down and open it immediately.

Let me expand on this last point. It is my own opinion based on 55 years of shotgun shooting, that unfired guns should be opened immediately. However, there are governing and advisory bodies that stipulate the gun should not be opened for 30 seconds in case of a delayed ignition of the primary propellant.

There are also rules governing clay target competitions that in the event of a misfire the gun must not be opened until the referee is in a position to check it. The referee is checking that the shooter has not forgotten to put the safety catch in the 'off position' prior to calling for the target(s).

To sum up: Use your own commonsense judgement and adhere to all governing and local competition and safety rules.

Killing a clay with a live cartridge

Time to kill your first clay. Pick up the gun, open it, and check that the barrels are clear. I have loaded one cartridge. Close the gun, keep your trigger finger outside the trigger guard resting alongside the action.

Mount the gun comfortably into your cheek and shoulder, and point at the kill point, wind the barrels back to the pick up point, and call "pull". Point at the clay, move with it, push in front and fire. Gun down and open. Great – your first kill! Try another, just repeat the process.

Try a few more. You missed a couple by forgetting to push in front. Everyone does that when they begin to learn to shoot. Making the lead picture is the only part of the Method that is initially alien to the eyes and brain.

Remember your strongest, most natural urge is to shoot at the target - your shotgun is a weapon and the clay is a target. Everyone knows that 'weapons' are aimed at targets! Beginning with the games we play as children our brains become trained to aim at things that we wish to strike or hit.

Don't worry; with a little bit of practice it soon becomes more natural to make a lead picture as you shoot.

Don't think about the odd clays that you missed. Enjoy the ones you kill!

Killing a single driven clay

The next target is a single driven clay – the trajectory is different. This time the clay will appear about 80 yards in front of you and will travel towards you to pass over your head about 50 feet above you. The Method is the same, but the pictures are slightly different.

Your feet position allows you to face the spot where the clay appears, as it is coming straight towards you. Your best kill point is up in front of you at an angle of about 70° – 80°.

You pick up the target and move with it just as before. The crucial difference here is that as you push in front of the clay you will of course lose sight of it, as it will have become obscured from view by the barrels and remainder of the gun. It is losing sight of the clay that tells you that it is time to fire. We call this 'blotting out' the target. Again, it will be achieved by a controlled acceleration – that 'gentle push with the left hand'.

First, a practice on a few targets with the gun empty.

You may find that the eyes and brain are initially reluctant to lose sight of the target. Remember, 'push and blot it out'!

As you set up for this target, lean into the gun to take your weight well forward. You will prevent the weight of the gun forcing you backwards as you point at the approaching clay if you straighten your right leg and raise the right heel.

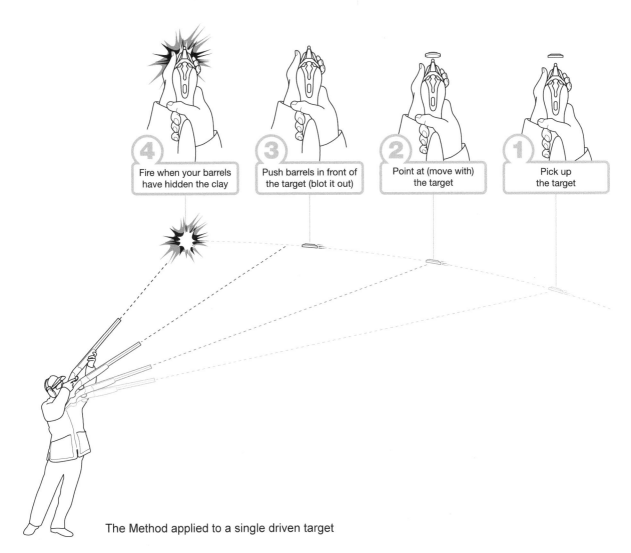

4	**3**	**2**	**1**
Fire when your barrels have hidden the clay	Push barrels in front of the target (blot it out)	Point at (move with) the target	Pick up the target

The Method applied to a single driven target

Now to kill some driven clays. Mount the gun comfortably into the cheek and shoulder pocket. Set the barrels on the pick up point. Call "pull". Pick up the target, move with it, push to blot it out and fire! Actually, say the word 'push' silently in your head as you shoot. At the same time discipline yourself to feel the comb of the stock pressing into your cheek.

That is good, you have killed your first driven target, now enjoy killing some more. Slow down between shots, there is no need to rush. Be comfortable then concentrate hard as you call 'pull'. Comfort, concentration and confidence are essential for successful shooting.

Don't let a few misses frustrate you, but let me tell you what caused you to miss some driven targets that you were sure you could kill. When you missed, your cheek was away from the comb, your head had lifted off the stock. Remember those very strong natural urges to aim at the target? Add to those urges the normal mental objection to deliberately losing sight of the very object that you are trying to strike. You can add a third strong urge to the previous two: Your very strong desire to continue your success. You know you can strike that clay, so you naturally want a good view of doing so!

The 'wrong master eye'

Now I will show you the effect of a left master eye for a right-handed shooter.

I will firstly fire one shot from 25 yards, at the mark in the centre of the Pattern Plate with my left eye shut. See how the shot has struck the point of aim. Now I will simulate a left master eye, by closing my right eye. My left eye is telling my brain that the gun is still pointing at the centre of the plate. Let's see what happens when I shoot. The shot pattern has hit the left hand side of the plate. This is the result of the left eye pulling the gun across the body to line up with the end of the barrels.

The wrong master eye is a very common phenomenon among shotgun shooters. Most cope with it very easily by learning to squint or close that eye. Those that do not feel comfortable doing so can easily solve the problem by wearing a pair of glasses with the master eye lens diffused so that the wrong eye cannot focus on the target.

My practical experiences have taught me to expect that about 40% of male and 90% of female pupils have the wrong master eye.

There are also some right-handed pupils who just prefer to shut their left eye when pointing at a clay target (vice versa for left-handers). Providing that they are pick-

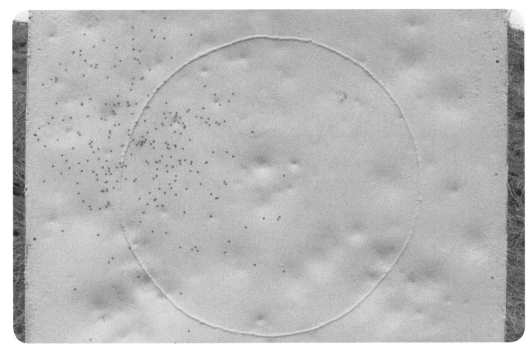

Plate showing the pattern of a right-handed left-eye-dominant shooter keeping the left eye open

ing up the target with both eyes open, I encourage this group to carry on doing what they are comfortable with.

Those of us who are lucky enough to be able to shoot successfully with both eyes open of course benefit from the advantage of retaining binocular vision. Two eyes probably send more efficient (natural) optical signals to the brain. Despite the real advantages of shooting with both eyes open, those who need or want to shoot with one eye shut should be encouraged to do so.

It really is time that the ridiculously old fashioned and misplaced dogmatic 'must have both eyes open' is dispensed with.

What to do before your next lesson

Well done, you have finished your first shooting lesson. You have learned to shoot the Method on a single crossing and single driven target; safely, competently and without discomfort.

During the next lesson you will shoot some crossing targets at greater distances so that you can begin to assess necessary changes in the lead picture. You will also shoot targets crossing left to right and be introduced to shooting doubles.

Before you go, a few words about equipment. You are now hugely enthusiastic about your new exciting hobby, which is great. Your very normal inclination will be to dash out to buy your new gun and all the kit. Hold back on buying the gun. Firstly, you will almost certainly move up at least one calibre and we have plenty of guns that will be comfortable for you to shoot during your lessons. Secondly, you are much more likely to know what style of gun you prefer when you have had more gun handling and shooting experience. You can however plan ahead and start acquiring equipment. Just think how happy your family and friends will be when they don't have to wrack their brains about presents for you, because you have given them a long list!

High on your planning ahead list is your shotgun certificate application. I will give you an application form before you leave. Also your shotgun security cabinet, because when the police are processing your application they will visit and of course check out your gun security.

You will need four passport style photographs to accompany your certificate application, one which will have to be signed by your counter signatory person named on your application. The form explains what status that person must have.

We will provide all the equipment necessary for your safety and comfort but you might like to make a list of other items that you will need.

Shooting safety glasses are compulsory when you shoot with me. They are essential for protecting your eyes from clay fragments, but also the ultra violet lenses and tints will enhance your vision in varying light conditions. We provide yellow for dull conditions and black for bright sunshine. You may choose to be more sophisticated and buy glasses with a variety of lens colours.

Earmuffs are again compulsory when you shoot with me. They are essential for your long-term hearing protection, but also greatly improve your comfort. Some people prefer earplugs that will protect your eardrums from the high frequency bang of the gun. However, only earmuffs that completely cover your ears will provide long-term hearing protection!

I am providing you with passive muffs, but you might prefer to invest in electronic ones like mine - full hearing protection from high frequency blasts but added comfort by being able to hear voice and other low frequency background noises naturally.

Hearing protection and shooting safety glasses are mandatory if you are participating in a registered shooting competition.

Now what about that present list:

• A shooting hat, something with a stiff front and a peak. Not compulsory, but I strongly recommend one. The obvious protection from falling pieces of clay and also protection from hot sun or cold, wet conditions. The peak will also reduce the glare of fierce sunlight.

• A shooting vest and in due course maybe a long sleeved waterproof version for winter conditions.

• A cartridge bag, which could be one designed to hold cartridges in boxes or loose cartridges. They are normally leather and can be designed to match your fancy leather gun slip! I don't know how generous your family is!

• A lightweight waterproof suit and heavier waterproof coat plus comfortable waterproof footwear.

These will do for now, but you of course can make the list as long as you like.

When you do eventually acquire your own gun, you will need a cleaning kit which is often included free of charge by your generous local gun shop along with a basic gun slip.

There is one other very important addition to your list of preparation for clay shooting: You really should be in possession of public liability shooting insurance as all responsible shooters are.

The easiest route to insurance cover is via membership of one of the shooting associations. Your choice, but logically if you think you might progress to field or game shooting, then enrol with either The Countryside Alliance or the British Association of Shooting and Conservation. Conversely, if you feel that your pleasure will be solely clay target shooting then enrol with the C.P.S.A.

Notes on the 'follow through'

Experienced shots, and certainly other CPSA coaches, will notice the omissions from the text and diagrams of the term 'follow through'. This is deliberate but of course deserves a full explanation.

Many years ago I was introduced to the CPSA method on a CPSA Club Coaching course. I was an immediate and enthusiastic convert to this wonderfully simple system of teaching beginners to shoot clays. The CPSA method included 'follow through' as the final movement of the gun; which I followed slavishly for many years; indeed I regret to say it appears in print in the original edition of this book published in 1991.

Thankfully, I continue to learn and a few years ago it occurred to me that 'follow through' was an unnatural and unnecessary movement: Yes, the gun is kept moving at the time of squeezing the trigger; however, I now believe that if the method is adhered to the gun will follow through naturally.

Here is my logic: When the gun is pointed at a moving target it is naturally moving at the appropriate relative speed. If the relative movement of the gun is speeded up to make the correct kill picture (the push) and the trigger is squeezed on the recognition of that picture; the gun must come to a gradual and natural stop.

In simple terms the 'follow through' has happened naturally.

While I continually hear "I/he/she stopped the gun", it is my opinion that rarely does anyone stop the gun. However I do understand why people think that they have.

When attempting to make a kill picture it is a common adult reaction to try to make the picture precisely correct. This often results in a fractional moment's hesitation. Conscious intelligence is checking the kill picture. I call this 'playback time'; hardly measurable, but enough to cause a miss behind the target.

If you are a novice pupil, or maybe you are an experienced shooter trying to help a beginner, I would encourage you to forget 'follow through'. Focus on squeezing the trigger on recognition of the correct kill picture. Trust the hands and avoid the precise approach. Remember kill pictures are always approximate.

Lesson Two
Extending the challenge

Welcome back for your second lesson. I am going to get you to shoot a few of the crossing targets that you started with on your first lesson.

The 20 Bore, and how to load it

From this lesson onwards I want you to load for yourself, and I will show you the simplest and most efficient way to do that shortly. Also, as you suffered no recoil effects to you shoulder or face during your first lesson, I am going to provide you with a 20 bore to use today.

This is the gun. It is the same make and size, and is exactly the same in operation as the 28 bore, although it will feel slightly heavier. You will still be comfortable with this gun because we have weighted the stock with 5oz of lead and fitted the most efficient butt recoil pad. As a further consideration to your comfort, you will be using a light load cartridge which is itself very low in recoil.

Now a couple of points on loading. The easiest way for you to load as a right-hander is by having loose cartridges in your left hand pocket. You will find that this requires fewer movements than trying to take cartridges from your right hand pocket with your right hand. This system of loading will also allow you to keep a continual hold of the grip of the gun with your natural holding hand (right hand). You will also be able to develop a nice simple, smooth loading rhythm.

Just go through the motions of loading a few times with the left hand from the left pocket using a snap cap.

You have a gun, cartridges, hat, earmuffs and shooting glasses, and I will show you one clay in flight before you start to shoot.

Here comes the first clay. Choose kill point, set feet, choose pick up point, now visualise and mentally rehearse the kill picture. For this particular target you will need to see a gap between the bead and the clay of about six inches.

Okay. Load, mount the gun, point at the kill point, wind back to the pick up point, call "pull", pick up the clay, move with it "push" and fire, gun down and open.

Well done. Kill a few more. Great! Five clays – five kills.

Lead Pictures for targets at greater distances

Now let's move back a few yards. Watch a clay in flight, now kill a few more.

This time you have missed a couple. Be aware that the target is now crossing further away from you. The shot has further to travel! Extend your lead picture. Try some more. Good. Now let's move back even further. Have a look at another clay in flight. Yes, it does seem a long way away, but you can kill it if you make the correct lead picture.

Try a few. Don't be frustrated by missing this clay. It was crossing 40 yards in front of you travelling at about 50/60 mph. At the moment your shot is missing behind and above the target. Remember 'point at' always means just underneath, make sure you see daylight between the bead and the clay.

This target just needs more lead, on the next one push in front until you see a lead picture that looks like you are going to miss about two feet ahead of the clay.

Try another one. "Push" hard! A kill! Well done. Very satisfying, isn't it? Shoot a few more. Okay, take a rest. Don't expect instant success on these more distant targets.

That type of target requires a great deal of practice. The gun and cartridges are perfectly adequate for killing clays at that range. It is the psychological difficulty that beats the shooter. Firstly, the distance looks daunting. Secondly, at that distance the clay appears to be travelling very slowly therefore sending messages via the eyes to the brain that little lead is required. Thirdly, the brain objects to moving barrels the large amount required in front of the target as it feels you are going to miss in front.

Just remember also that shooting a shotgun at a moving target is a totally primeval activity. Your shotgun is a weapon and the clay is a target, so of course you want to shoot at it.

To add to your frustration, the harder you concentrate on making that big lead picture, the more likely you are to hesitate before you squeeze the trigger.

You are already discovering the challenges of mastering new targets, and the pleasures of getting it right and killing them.

Left to Right targets

Let's go and look at a new target – the 'left to right' crossing target. This clay will appear from your left, come towards you, and pass in front and above you about 20 yards away, travelling to your right.

Try a few first and see how you get on. Harder than it looks, isn't it? However, the only extra difficulty of the left to right crosser is that it requires you to move the gun and your body in an unnatural movement. The target is flying against your natural body movement.

Firstly, you need to move your kill point further to your right. Straight in front of you at 90 degrees is ideal, as this is where you can assess lead most accurately. Now, remembering the 'clock' rule and that the kill point is 12 o'clock, place your feet at five-past-eleven. Now, as you wind back to the pick up point, you begin to

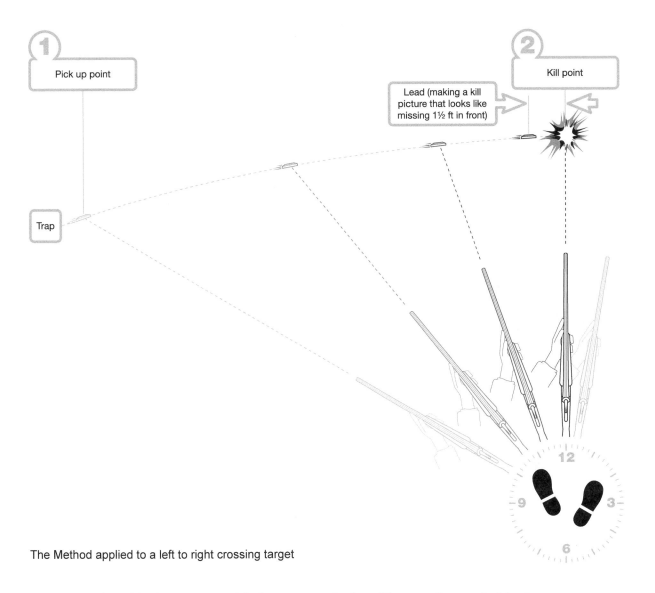

The Method applied to a left to right crossing target

feel uncomfortable, but put up with that as your body will naturally unwind back to the comfortable position dictated by your feet.

A few more tips on shooting this target successfully. Check your feet position every time you re-load. Because you are twisting your body back towards the pick up point, your feet will naturally want to turn in that direction. Lock the gun tightly into the soft part of your cheek. As the barrels have travelled to the kill point straight in front of you, and your left hand is now pushing them to your right to make the lead picture, there is a natural tendency to push the gun away from the face.

Lastly, give this target a bit more lead than you gave the first clay which crossed you right to left. Now try some more. You are still missing behind! Make a lead picture that looks like missing about one and a half feet in front. Now try some more. That is better, you are killing most of them. The keys to success on this target are making sure your feet are set to the correct position, a lead picture that looks a little too big, and locking the stock extra tightly into your cheek.

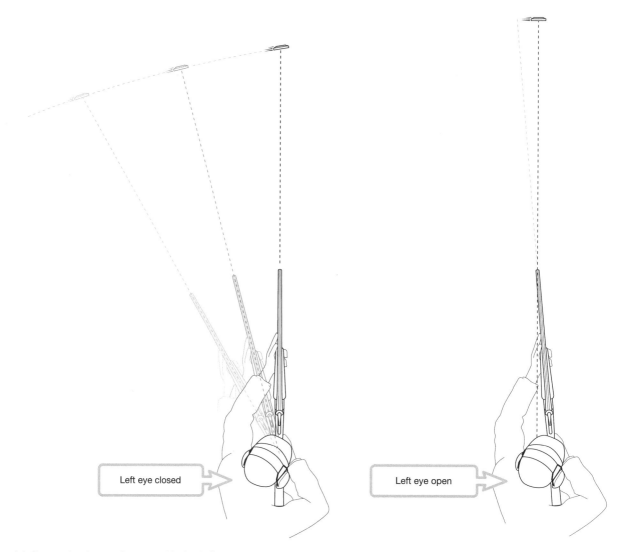

Left eye closed

Left eye open

A left-eye-dominant shooter with the left eye closed and the left eye open

Before we go onto doubles, a comment on a couple of the left to right crossing clays that you missed. You probably are not aware, but a couple were missed a long way behind. These misses were caused by your left eye opening which, being the dominant eye, took visual control of the gun and pulled the barrels to the left. It's just the opposite to pulling the barrels in front of the target when it was crossing right to left.

These will cease to be a problem when you have had more shooting experience. At the moment your left eye being your dominant eye wants to open whenever you are concentrating hard visually, ie making the correct lead picture.

The effect is shown effectively in a diagram, showing how keeping the left eye open pulls the gun away from a straight line.

More dramatically it can be seen by looking straight down the barrels of an empty shotgun held by someone with the left eye closed and open! (See picture overleaf).

You can practice shutting your left eye as you point at something that is moving when you are not shooting. Point at moving traffic, birds flying over the garden, movements on the television screen etc. Each time you point at a moving object, shut your left eye. You will be training the eye muscles to shut when your left hand points.

People seeing you doing this will of course assume you have gone quite dotty, but your shooting will improve tremendously!

Double targets

Take a rest while I explain the two most common types of doubles (or pairs) thrown in sporting clays.

Keeping the left eye closed with the gun stock locked into the cheek keeps the bead in line with the right eye.

Allowing the left eye to open pulls the barrel across to the shooter's left. Note - Safety Glasses have been removed for photographic purposes.

'Simultaneous pairs" or simultaneous doubles' is a self-explanatory term. Two clays are launched on the call of pull. 'On report pairs or doubles' describes the second clay being launched on the report of the gun being fired. Clays may be thrown from the same or from two separate traps.

You can try the 'on report' pair first. The target will be the right to left crosser, the same as in your first lesson, but a second clay will be launched from the same trap when you fire your gun at the first clay.

Before we begin. A safety reminder: You are about to be loading two cartridges in the gun. It is **crucial** that should the gun fail to fire the second barrel on the second squeeze of the trigger, open the gun immediately! Refer to my comments in Lesson One concerning what to do if the gun does not fire when you squeeze the trigger.

At the risk of stating the obvious, remember to release the trigger after the first shot, and then squeeze again to fire the second barrel.

Don't feel you have to rush your first shot, take your time. Treat all doubles as two separate singles.

Right. Load two cartridges and set yourself up ready to pick up the first clay. "Pull". You are killing the second clay consistently, but missing most of the first ones by rushing. Remember, the second clay is not launched until the report of the first shot, so you dictate how quickly the second clay comes. Kill both targets by shooting the Method. Concentrate 100% on the simple process of shooting the first clay. You must focus your mind solely on pointing at it, moving with it, pushing ahead and firing when you have made the correct lead picture. Then, and only then, wind back to the second target and repeat the same totally focussed approach. Try a few more. That is better. Treat these targets as two separate singles and suddenly this on report double seems much easier, doesn't it?

Take a breather and watch some of these simultaneous doubles. They are coming from the same trap position as the previous target and following the same flight path. Note that one clay is a few feet behind the other.

Your first decision on any simultaneous pair of clays is which one you will pick up and shoot first. In this case, the logical sequence will be the rear one first. The second clay will then be along the path of your natural right to left movement. In other words, as the barrels move in front of the first clay, it is the minimum of movement onto the second one.

You just need to discipline your eyes and brain to pick out the rear clay each time, and not think about the second clay until you have killed the first one.

Shoot the Method on the first target. Move the barrels onto the second target. Push in front, and fire the second barrel.

Yes, it is as easy as that! Go on, try some. Terrific. Ten clays, eight kills!

Don't look so surprised. Pupils invariably do well on the simultaneous doubles. It is an indication that your brain understands the principles of shooting more than you realise. On these doubles there is much more to do and less time to think, the result being that you shoot instinctively and therefore accurately.

You can finish the lesson by shooting simultaneous doubles as driven targets.

Here comes a pair for you to watch in flight. They are only a few feet apart, but as with all simultaneous doubles there is a logical target to be 'picked up' and shot first. Note that the clay on your right is slightly behind the left hand clay. Pick that one up first, so you will be moving your gun with the natural movement of your body from right to left. Also, as you are pointing the gun at targets coming towards you, your gun movement is of course upwards, so the second clay is along the path of the most natural movement of the gun.

Mental preparation

Watch a few more clays in flight and mentally visualise the pick up and kill points for both targets.

The process you are going through now is the same as for all the previous targets. It is known as 'reading the target'.

Whenever you are shooting clays, the initial mental preparation is always the same. First, the two most important decisions: Choosing the 'kill' and 'pick up' points, then setting your feet and body to the correct position. Most important: Before you call 'pull', close your eyes and visualise those lead pictures. See the clay in relation to the bead in your mind's eye - or in the case of the driven target, visualise the clay disappearing behind the barrels.

Remember, our brains love doing what is most familiar (comfortable) so the more we mentally rehearse the kill pictures, the more comfortable we are with them. The more comfortable you are with the lead pictures, the more likely you are to squeeze the trigger at the right moment.

Successful clay shooting mainly results from the mental preparation that you make before you call 'pull'.

In essence, you should be striving to 'stack the odds in your favour'. No targets should be considered easy until after you have killed them, but you should always be working to make them as easy as possible for you.

Technique for Driven Doubles

Now let us see how well you have prepared yourself for these driven doubles. You are doing well, but you would improve your kill ratio on the second target by killing the first one a little quicker. At the moment, you are shooting the second barrel as the clay is right above your head. There is always a tendency to do this

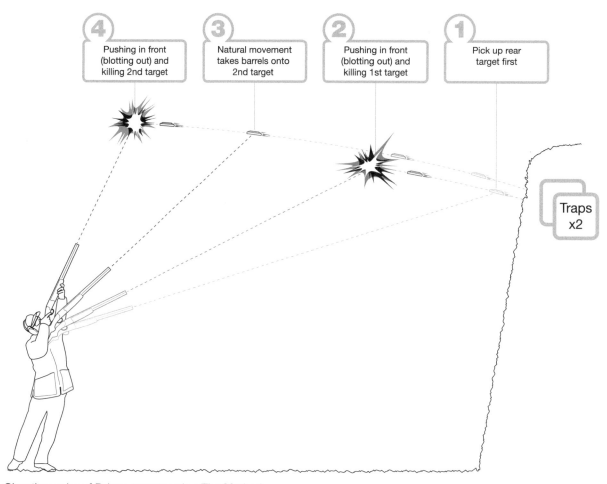

Shooting pairs of Driven targets using The Method

on driven targets as we are tempted by the psychological need to get the clays as close as possible before we shoot (the clays look bigger, therefore easier to kill.)

In reality, we have given ourselves real disadvantages if we fall to this temptation. Your normal intelligence drives you to 'make certain' to try extra hard to get it right. This results in spending too much time pointing at the first target.

There is another negative factor caused by the mesmerising effect of two clays moving close together. Your brain is starting to be comfortable with the process of focussing on one moving target. Now you have the distraction of a second moving target in your vision.

Only time and practice will result in consistent success on driven doubles, but you can now kill some by trying to shoot the first target a little sooner.

If you can kill the first clay between 60°- 70° and the second one at 70° - 80°, you will do very well. The further in front (the shallower the angle) you shoot, the lesser the effort required to move the barrels to 'blot out' the clay. Discipline yourself to shoot the clays earlier in their flight you will definitely kill more driven doubles.

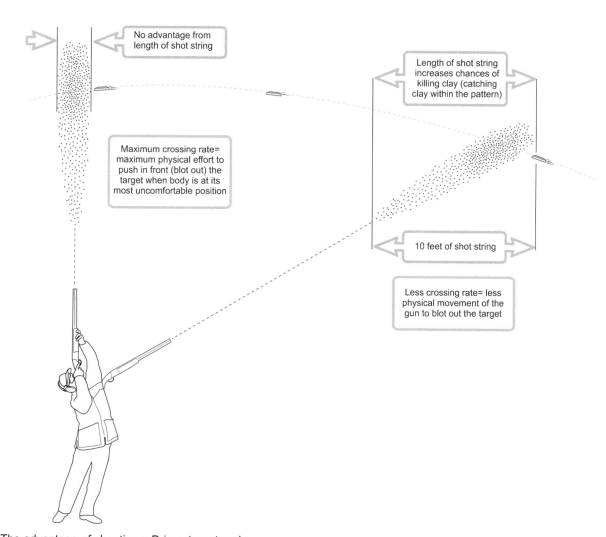

The advantage of shooting a Driven target early

Why is this? You will obviously have more time to shoot the second clay. You will also be more likely to keep your weight on your front foot, which will allow your torso to bend comfortably backwards as you will accelerate the gun upwards.

Conversely, consider the main disadvantages of shooting a clay straight above your head. The angle is 90° when the target moves fastest relative to you (maximum crossing rate) and your body - particularly your back - is at its most stretched and therefore least able to accelerate the gun.

Okay. Try again and be determined to kill both targets further in front. Blot out each of the clays and squeeze the trigger each time I shout 'push'. Well done! Pair killed! Now repeat that a few times. Say the word 'push' to yourself aggressively, to help you blot out the targets sooner. That is very good, you killed five pairs in succession. It is hard work to concentrate that much, but the reward is the pleasure of your success.

During your next lesson we will consolidate what you have already learned and teach you how to mount the gun.

How many more lessons should I take?

The most repeated question from complete beginners is, "how many lessons will I need?" I have yet to come up with a conclusive answer. Firstly, there is tremendous variance in the individual's learning ability that requires great flexibility in the teaching approach. Some require many lessons in a condensed period, some learn best by shooting a large number of targets, others might benefit from very gentle progress over an extended period. There are pupils who need private and individual attention, and their opposites who quickly shine in small groups from peer support and even in some cases peer pressure and competition.

If there is a general average of numbers of initial lessons required, it is around six. This is the number I would recommend to someone who participates in some form of clay shoot practice after the sixth lesson, by attending clay shoots, or to someone who has the facilities to practise privately with a few friends.

Typical fifth and sixth lessons are spent introducing the pupil to the various combinations of targets commonly encountered at sporting clay shoots. Most pupils who start from scratch with formal tuition return for lessons periodically. They might just need sharpening up, or be having difficulty with one particular target.

Which guns might I shoot?

The natural choice of gun for teaching beginners is the over and under, which I use in 28, 20 and 12 bore calibres, including 20 and 12 bores that have been recoil reduced by adding some lead to the stock (3 oz – 6 oz, or 85 – 170g) depending on the actual weight of the gun. The increase in weight behind the action simply dampens down the force caused by the gun firing. The felt recoil is also reduced by fitting the most efficient recoil reducing butt pad. This pad also greatly reduces the likelihood of the butt slipping in the shoulder. Some guns also have cheek pads fitted to the combs of stocks to reduce the felt shock wave to the cheek.

Whilst I choose not to use them, there are also various types of mechanical recoil reducers that can be fitted into stocks.

The 28 bore is used most commonly for youngsters and ladies. The gun has been cut down in size to reduce weight, but retains very low recoil properties, as there are far fewer pellets in a 28 bore compared to a 12 bore cartridge, and a much smaller charge is required to propel them. The lighter the propellant charge, the less the recoil.

Regardless of calibre, all tuition guns have little or no choking in order that the pattern of shot is as wide as possible.

A pupil who has the physical stature to hold and shoot a 12 bore comfortably will of course have more chance of connecting with the clays than a pupil using a

This 12 Bore is too long and heavy for a person of this physique

smaller calibre. The pattern from the 12 bore will be wider as the pellets have been discharged from a tube of greater diameter. However, the choice is always dictated by comfort requirements. Many pupils who begin shooting with a smaller calibre often progress to using a larger one.

To put this into some perspective, from the last ten pupils who began to shoot with a 28 bore, five are now using a 12 bore, four are using a 20 bore and one has stayed with the 28 bore.

Once a pupil has fired enough cartridges to convince them that there is no pain associated with firing the gun, they tend to relax and cease to be aware of recoil.

Quite often someone who has been shooting for a while will take shooting lessons because they are suffering from bruising to the shoulder and face. I try to encourage them to use a gun of a smaller calibre than their own for a short period. Once their subconscious has ceased to worry about recoil I am quickly able to show them the source of the original discomfort and provide the solution to it. Invariably, it will have been caused by poor gun fit or incorrect gun mounting.

Correct gun mounting will be covered in the next lesson.

Lesson Three
Mounting the gun

During this lesson I am going to teach you 'gun mounting' and then get you to practice it on targets similar to the ones that you have already been introduced to.

Essentials of gun mounting

Gun mounting is the co-ordinated movements of placing the shotgun into the cheek and shoulder whilst simultaneously picking up, pointing at and moving with the clay target.

The objectives of good gun mounting are to ensure that the stock is taken to exactly the same (and correct) position in your cheek and shoulder every time you fire the gun, to make certain that there is a straight line from your right eye to where the shot is to be placed, and also that you do not experience discomfort from recoil. Finally, the physical movements should be as natural and minimal as possible.

You might logically ask why not always start with the gun ready mounted? The reasons are:

• When you mount the gun into your shoulder and cheek, you tense the muscles of your arms, neck and shoulders.
• Also, once the gun is mounted you have lost full peripheral (and therefore natural) vision.

These two factors combined prevent you from reacting with your best natural eye, brain and body efficiency.

You were encouraged to shoot the targets in the first two lessons with the gun ready mounted for a number of very good reasons, the most important of which is to learn and relate to the pictures of the Method as quickly and simply as possible. This resulted in you killing clays very early in your learning process, which in turn increased your confidence.

You have been helped to place the stock in the proper cheek and shoulder positions, so you have not suffered from recoil, and also now know instinctively what the correct gun mount feels like.

Technique for mounting from the gun down position

The most important factor to retain is that a right-hander should start the gun mount movements with the **left** hand! The simple and natural movements begin from the 'gun ready' position, which I will demonstrate.

My hands are holding the gun at the grip and forend in exactly the same way as when it is mounted. However, the stock has now been dropped so that it is just level, and a little forward of my hip with the butt visible below my elbow. The ends of the barrels are pointed at the pick up point. My eyes are now focused in that direction using the bead as a reference point. If I have placed the barrels correctly, I will see the target instantly sat on the bead. I will have achieved the quickest, simplest and most natural 'pick up'.

As I see the clay, my left hand pushes and points the barrel at it in flight. This natural pointing and pushing action of the left hand and arm achieves two simultaneous benefits: The barrels maintain contact with the clay, and as the gun is pushed away from the body the stock is taken forwards and upwards towards the cheek and shoulder.

1 - The Gun Ready position. The left hand points at the clay as it comes into view.

2 - The left hand tracks the target, the right hand brings the stock towards the cheek.

3 - The gun stock is brought into the cheek and locked in tightly.

4 - The left hand pushes the barrels in front of the target, while the right hand keeps the stock locked into the cheek and fires. Note that the weight is well forward on the front foot.

At this first stage of the mount the right hand does no more than carry the stock to follow the movement of the left hand. The right hand and arm exert no deliberate physical effort until the left arm has pushed forward to a natural pointing position. The stock will have been taken about two thirds of the way to the mounted position. All the right hand now needs do is pull the stock into the cheek and shoulder. Note that I kept my head upright with my right eye always in line with the end of the barrels. The comb comes up into the cheek – **not** cheek down onto comb.

The 'gun ready' position and first movements of the left hand facilitate the first stages of the Method (pick up and point at). As the gun is locked into the mounted position, the movement with the clay is maintained until it is time to push in front and fire!

A lot of words to explain what is actually a very simple and natural movement.

Take the empty gun and adopt the 'gun ready' position. Relax your arms whilst I move the gun from ready to mounted position. Feel how naturally the stock comes up to the shoulder!

Now I want you to shoot some driven single targets, starting from the gun down position. Take a few dry runs with the gun empty.

Decide kill point, feet position, pick up point. Take up the gun ready position with the barrels on the pick up point. Now call for a few clays and mount the gun on them. Look for the clay with both eyes open, then just squint your left eye as you push and point the barrels at it. You must start with both eyes open in order to retain full and natural vision.

An exercise to encourage the correct use of the left hand while gun mounting

62

Careful! You are snatching and rushing the stock into your shoulder as soon as you see the target. If you relax and use your left hand first, you will discover that you have plenty of time. Before you shoot any of these targets, I am going to take you through a little exercise to encourage you to use your left hand.

Developing the left hand

Take up the 'gun ready' position again. Now take your right hand off the stock. I know the gun feels awkward but you are quite capable of holding it. Call for a few more clays and do nothing more than push and point the barrels at them. Good. That is exactly how I want you to start the gun mount. Practice mounting on a few more clays with the empty gun. Easy, isn't it? Shoot a few. Stop! You have missed the first three clays although you have mounted the gun quite correctly.

Your shot missed in front! Don't worry; you have actually discovered another advantage of starting from the gun down (ready) position and beginning the mount by pointing and pushing the left hand.

Let me explain what is happening by reminding you of things I have said previously. Remember, when you see the moving target appear, without the gun in your shoulder you have normal vision, therefore your reactions are more spontaneous. You are simply pointing naturally at something that is moving. This first instinctive movement actually results in the barrels moving with whatever momentum is required to keep in line (pointing at the clay). This momentum greatly reduces the need for such an aggressive 'push in front'.

To shoot a driven clay at this height and speed, you do no more than squeeze the trigger as you lose sight of it! Just a gentle speed up of the movement (a little push) with the left hand, blot it out and fire.

Try a few more. Very good. Relax while we move onto the crossing target.

Set up, gun ready, barrels on the pickup point. Call for your target. That is okay, but every few shots you tend to let your right hand take over. If you lift the stock straight into your shoulder with your right hand, your left hand will act as a fulcrum, resulting in the ends of the barrels dipping downwards. When this happens, the clay is no longer sat on top of the bead and you must then put in extra effort to rush the barrels back onto the clay, generally resulting in firing the gun past the comfortable kill point when the natural movement of the body slows down, causing you to miss behind.

Make the left hand kill the target, because that is the hand that is pointing the barrels (placing the shot) where you want it. The right hand is only needed to lock the stock into the cheek and shoulder, and squeeze the trigger.

Let's talk through the whole sequence once more. Kill point, feet, gun ready with barrels on the pick up point. Focus both eyes on the pick up point. "Pull", pick up the target, squint your left eye. Push the barrels towards the clay and keep pointing at it. Lock the stock into the cheek and shoulder, push in front as the barrels approach the kill point, make the lead picture and fire. Gun down and open it.

Kill some clays! Good shooting!

Mounting for double targets

Now, shoot the same clays but 'on report'. Remember, they are two separate singles!

When you are ready, call for the clays in your own time. That is fine, you have no particular problems with these targets. However, you are not dismounting the gun after killing the first clay!

Now that you have practised mounting the gun, you have discovered that it is actually much easier than calling for the target with the gun ready mounted: Better vision, more relaxed, more natural, more time and less tiring. You are actually making the second target more difficult than it need be. Remember, you should always be trying to make each shot as easy as possible.

Try a few more pairs, but dismount the gun after you have killed your first target. Simply drop the stock with your right hand, whilst your left hand takes the barrels back to the pick up point. That is better, and much easier, wasn't it?

You will see the benefit of dismounting the gun between shots on the next targets which will be on report doubles, but this time from two separate traps. On the call of pull, the first clay is the driven target that you were shooting earlier. On the report of the gun, the second target will appear on your left crossing to your right and passing in front of you about 25 yards away. I will show you both targets a few times.

Okay. Let's see how you get on.

The first target is no problem, is it? However, you are having trouble with the second one. Can you recall the mental preparation we talked about earlier (reading the target)? Watch a few more of the on report clays.

Firstly, it is a 'left to right crosser' – it is going to need more effort than the first target. So your first consideration is your feet position. It is always a compromise in these situations – but as a rule of thumb, you stack the odds in your favour by setting your feet to the kill point of the more difficult target.

Secondly, to give yourself a little more time to pick up the crossing target, choose a pick up further along its flight path, ie further right than you are doing at the moment. You are simply trying to make it as easy as possible for your left hand to take the barrels from the kill point of the first clay to the pick up point of the second one.

Thirdly, the second target is going to need more lead than the first.

Finally, you will find that your left eye opens naturally as you take the barrels down to pick up the second target. This means you will pick it up more easily, but do not forget to close the eye again as you start to make the pictures of the Method. You will be concentrating very hard so the 'master eye' will want to stay open.

Right, mentally rehearse the sequence and pictures for both targets, then set yourself up for shooting. A last reminder: Shoot these targets as **two separate** singles – do not think about the second clay until you have killed the first one!

Call when you are ready. Excellent! You should be very pleased with those last kills. That is enough shooting for one lesson – you deserve a rest.

A brief look at the traps

You have seen the clays appearing at various angles. Perhaps you would like to have a look at a couple of the clay traps that are throwing them.

From a safety point of view, note that the throwing arms are visible sticking out at 90° from the traps. That tells us that these traps are disarmed.

During the next lesson I will be introducing you to some different Sporting Clay targets.

An automatic clay target trap. Note that the throwing arm is sticking out to the left to show that the trap is disarmed and therefore safe.

A clay is launched from an automatic trap. For safety's sake, **always approach a trap from the rear!**

The Mini, Midi and Standard clay targets

An assortment of Blaze clay targets

Lesson Four

Typical Sporting Clay targets

So far we've looked at crossing targets and driven targets. During this lesson I am going to introduce you to some other common Sporting Clay targets. The difference between them lies in their starting point and trajectory. It is of course impossible to turn you into an expert on any of them in just a few lessons, but you will have had the experience of shooting them, and I will have been able to have shown you the easiest ways to tackle each one.

Overhead targets

We will start with the Overhead target. This clay is thrown from the trap position behind and above you, travelling in the direction that you are facing. As usual, the first exercise is to watch a few clays in flight. Right, now let's compare this to the other types of targets that you have shot, and decide on the best way to approach it.

As you call 'pull', you hear the trap go off and then seem to have a long wait until the clay appears up ahead of you. The first difficulties are psychological ones. Firstly, there's the delay between 'pull' and the clay coming into your area of vision, since with all previous targets the clays have appeared instantly. Your first reactive impressions are of the speed of the target and lack of time to shoot it. The previous targets have all been approaching you, albeit at different angles, and the clays have looked bigger as they become nearer. Now the clay seems to rapidly diminish in size as it speeds away from you. Time for the necessary decisions now. Kill point, pick up point, feet and gun ready position.

You should try to kill this clay as soon as you can comfortably do so. You will discover that this target will appear to be travelling in a straight line away from you and will induce a tendency to 'aim' the gun straight at it. Your pick up and gun ready/body position are going to be the key to success on this target. Only by

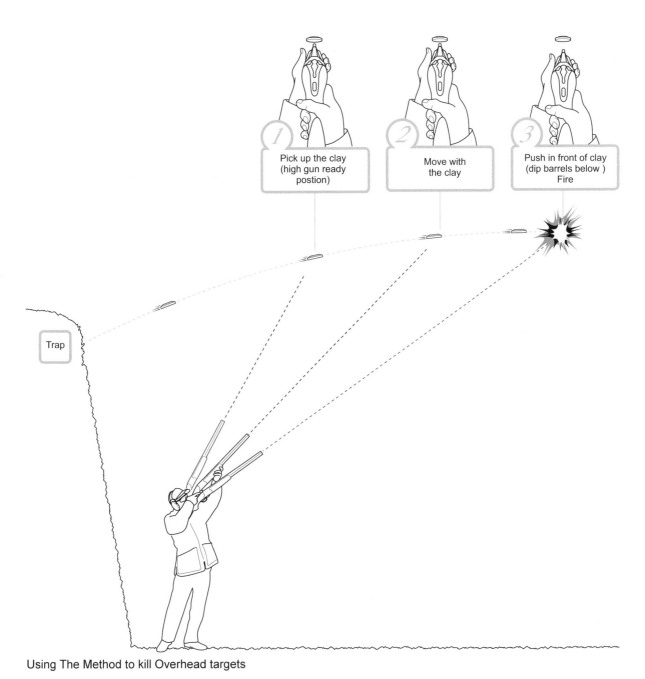

1 — Pick up the clay (high gun ready postion)

2 — Move with the clay

3 — Push in front of clay (dip barrels below) Fire

Trap

Using The Method to kill Overhead targets

69

picking up the target early will you be able to have time to shoot the Method and make the lead picture whilst the target's actual relative movement is obvious.

The gun ready position that you adopted for driven and crossing targets will not allow you sufficient time to shoot this target; it will be about 40 yards away and dropping rapidly from its flight path by the time you have the gun mounted.

Let me demonstrate the gun ready and pick up: Feet facing the kill point out in front of me, weight well forward onto the front foot. The barrels are lifted until they are almost vertical, then push upward until the butt is just below the arm pit. Now the head is canted backwards so that the straight line from right eye; through the bead, to pick up point, is achieved. Now the gun will be pointed at the target much, much sooner.

It is that same initial point and push at the target that will make the shot natural. The barrels will automatically move with the correct momentum. As the barrels are pushed at and with the target, the stock is taken naturally into the cheek and shoulder pocket, simply then to be locked into position by the right hand. When the gun is locked into the mounted position, the barrels are taken in front of the clay to make the lead picture, which in this case looks as though you are shooting beneath it. The push in front feels like dipping the barrels to point under the clay.

The sequence of the Method is just the same: Point at, move with, push in front and fire. An aggressive initial point with the left hand is very important on this target. As soon as the gun is locked into the cheek and shoulder and you can see daylight between the barrels and the clay – squeeze the trigger!

Let me help you with the gun ready position. Take up the ready position, now push upwards and lean your head backwards so that you are ready to pick up the target with the barrels. Keep your weight on your left foot and bend back from the waist. I know you are feeling uncomfortable whilst you try and familiarise your-

70

self but when you are actually shooting you will only be holding this position for a fraction of a second. As you call 'pull' you will have that bonus of your body wanting to unwind back to a comfortable position.

It is time for you to shoot a few. Just prepare yourself mentally for pointing the barrels at the clay with the left hand. Call 'pull'. Good. First clay – first kill. Now shoot some more like that!

Careful! Now you are missing behind the target (your shot is passing over the top of the clay).

Rather than waste mental energy on 'do nots', here is a reminder of some important 'do's!

Gun Ready position for an Overhead target

• Do bring the barrels and head as far back as you comfortably can.
• Do make sure that your first movement of this gun mount is the 'point and push' at the clay with the left hand.
• Do make sure that the stock comb stays locked into the cheek, to prevent you from lifting your head to take a better look at the target.
• Do keep your weight over your left foot.
• Do shoot as soon as the barrels move in front of the clay (fire as soon as there is daylight between the bead and the underside of the clay).

Shoot some more. That is very good, that particular gun ready position is very tiring but you now know how to stack the odds in your favour on this target.

The Bolting Rabbit

Onto something different: The Bolting Rabbit. A special clay with a wider levelled rim to enable it to be rolled along the ground. The clay will appear on your left about 25 yards away, cross 90° in front of you, and disappear behind the bank on your right.

Look for the clay appearing on your left. Very fast, isn't it? Perhaps 'hurtling' is a better description than rolling! Let us recognise the difficulties and then decide how to cope best with them. Firstly, the speed. It looks faster than the clays moving in the air because there is an actual close physical background that its movement is seen and instantly measured against. Secondly, there is an extra impres-

Gun Ready position for a Bolting Rabbit

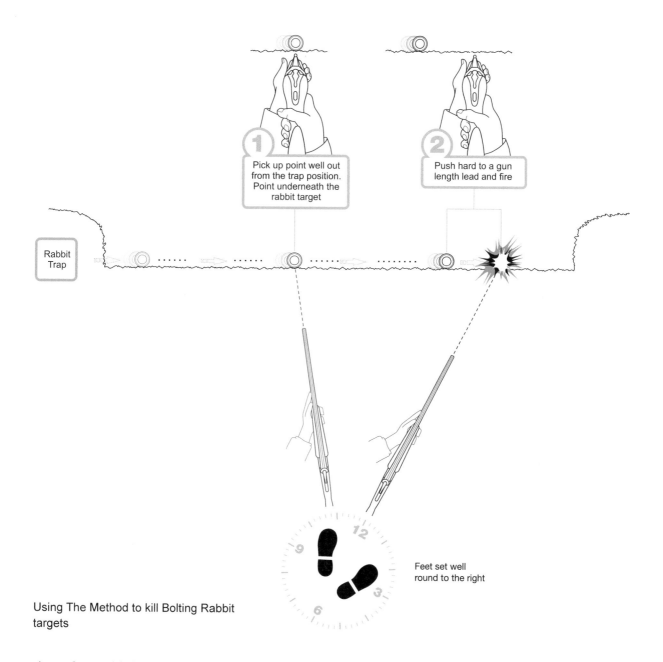

1 Pick up point well out from the trap position. Point underneath the rabbit target

2 Push hard to a gun length lead and fire

Rabbit Trap

Feet set well round to the right

Using The Method to kill Bolting Rabbit targets

sion of very high speed because it is in view for such a short time. The distance from where it appears to the point where it becomes obscured by the bank is only about 20 yards.

You can use the Method to kill the Bolting Rabbit but you must mentally shorten the sequence.

An accurate pick up is crucial: There is no time for readjustment! To shorten the Method sequence, you literally start your push in front as soon as you have picked up the target, and keep pushing the barrels until they are about two feet in front of it.

You will be trying to kill the rabbit when it is about two yards from that bank.

If you find that your barrels are far enough before that point, shoot! The quicker you shoot the better. The more instinctively you can react, the greater your accuracy. Now set up and try some. Remember, it is moving left to right, so make sure you set your feet well round that way. You will be shooting downwards, so you must lean forward with most of your weight over your left foot. Take up a gun ready position that has the gun nearly mounted. Just hold the gun far enough out of your shoulder to allow you to see naturally.

When the rabbit appears, point the barrels at it with the left hand. Lock the stock into your cheek and shoulder, and start pushing in front. Remember to lock in extra tight to your cheek because this is a left to right target.

Let us see how you get on. No luck so far, you are missing a long way behind. Try not to let the speed of the target frighten you. Just see it as another clay target that you can kill if you point the barrels far enough in front. The lead picture here is as big as the one you used effectively on the long crosser during the second lesson. In that situation, the lead was necessary because of distance. Here, it is needed because of the relative speed of the target (ie fast crossing rate) and it is moving left to right.

Concentrate, and be as determined and aggressive as you can. Add an extra dimension to your mental image of the lead: Imagine that you must squeeze the trigger to ensure that your shot is placed a full two feet in front of the target. Have another go! Great! You have killed some. Now take a rest.

It is important that the barrels are pointed a little below the level of the clay, for two reasons. Firstly, the clay is more visible and secondly, that any ricochet of the pellets will add to the chances of the clay being broken.

The Going Away

Your next target is the Going Away target. The trap is immediately in front of you the other side of that earth mound. On the call of 'pull' the clay travels directly away from you. There it goes!

Your reactions are probably similar to when you saw the first overhead target: Speed, lack of time, and the clay looking more and more difficult as it diminishes in size with distance.

Before you shoot it, let me give you a few reminders to help you make it as easy as possible.

The clay appears to be travelling along a straight flat line away from you, so there will be a tendency to 'aim' the gun once it is mounted. If you do aim the gun, it will be static as you shoot. Also, aiming will cause you to wait too long before you shoot, by which time the clay will be flattening out on its trajectory, or even dropping. Remember, shooting a shotgun at a moving target is just like pointing the left fore finger. 'Point at it and shoot' and you are home and dry!

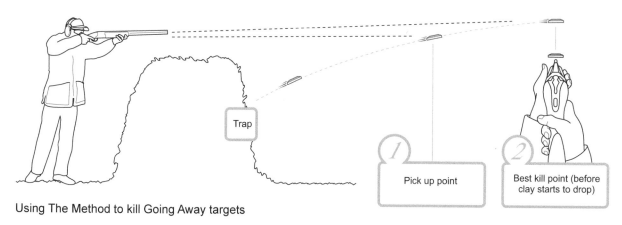

Trap

Pick up point

Best kill point (before clay starts to drop)

Using The Method to kill Going Away targets

Gun Ready position for a Going Away target

Okay. Try a few. Don't worry about missing. The speed of this going away target is simply causing you to rush your gun mount, so change your gun ready position to pre-mounted.

The rules of Sporting Clays allow for an optional gun ready position. Many clay shots approach any type of going away target with their guns pre-mounted. Make sure that the barrels are on your chosen earliest pick up point. Concentrate fully on that area, and as soon as the target appears point and push the barrels at it.

Somewhere out along the flight path of that clay there is an imaginary line. Whilst the clay is this side of the line, your eyes and brain are pointing instinctively (accurately). Once that clay has passed that line you have started to point consciously and are most likely to aim (to try and make certain). Forget the gun for a moment. When do you ever point at something instinctively without pointing straight at it?

For the next few clays I want you to just point at the bird and squeeze the trigger instantly I shout "shoot!".

Five clays, five kills! I was simply looking over your shoulder at the bead and trusting your eyes, and your ability to point.

Now you try it. Trust your reactions and shoot quickly. That is very good. Shoot some on report doubles. Remember to concentrate 100% on the first target, and don't give any thought to the second target until you have killed the first one. However, when you have shot the first clay, take the barrels quickly back to the pick up point so that you are ready for the 'on report' clay.

Trust your hands, just let them go! If you keep your head locked tight and sit the clays just above the bead, you can't miss! You do not have time to dismount the gun. Shoot quickly and instinctively. Very good! It's the perfect practice for the Springing Teal target, which we will introduce in your next lesson.

Lesson Five
More Sporting Clay Targets

The Springing Teal

Today we will start with the Springing Teal, very similar to the going away target that you finished your last lesson on.

We will look at singles, then doubles, from two traps elevated to about 70°. Neither the going away target or the springing target can be shot using the Method in full, as you cannot physically give lead to a clay travelling straight away from you, and of course if you blot it out you are likely to miss above it.

The single 'Springing Teal' is particularly difficult to follow; increasing height is added to increasing distance. Use this appearance of great speed by reacting to it! Start with the gun pre-mounted. As the clay appears from under the barrels, push them hard to keep them pointing at it and squeeze the trigger as soon as you have the clay sat just above the bead. Make sure you see all of the clay as you shoot. See the 'kill picture' as being the bottom edge of the clay just above the bead. Shoot some singles. Stop a minute. You have the barrels too high at the gun ready position, causing the clay to be hidden by the gun for too long. The sooner you can be pointing at this clay, the sooner you can kill it, but be careful not to drop the barrels too low, or you will be wasting time chasing the clay where it is travelling fastest. Try again.

That is good, now we will shoot the doubles. These need careful reading. See how they climb rapidly then suddenly seem to run out of steam and hang in mid-air just for a fraction of time before they drop to the ground. There is a natural

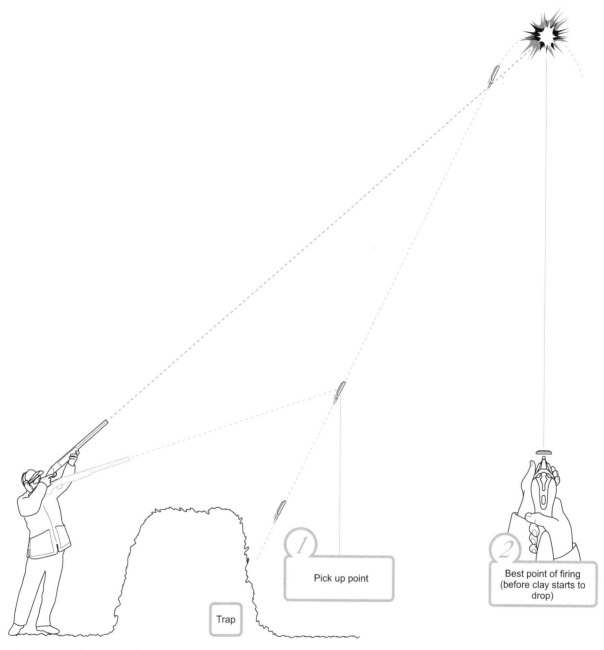

1 Pick up point

Trap

2 Best point of firing (before clay starts to drop)

Using The Method to kill Springing Teal targets

temptation to wait until they seem to be slowing down or hanging in the air and look so easy. The reality is that a very slow (apparently stationary) target causes us to shoot with a static gun. Shoot the clay that is slowing down soonest first, just like the single, then move the barrels straight over to the second target and make a kill picture that has the bead about twice as far underneath as you had it for the first target pair. Try not to be tempted to wait until they are slowing down. If you can get the timing right, you should catch the second clay just as it is reaching the top of its flight, or its zenith. Shoot some. Well shot, the only one you missed was on the first pair when you were tempted to wait too long on the second clay.

The Dropping Clay

I am going to show this one to you straight away as a double, as this is generally how it is presented at Sporting Clay shoots.

These are pairs of Dropping Clays. The clays could be presented from various angles. However, these are being thrown from two traps a long way away from this shooting position. I am going to use traps that will throw clays towards you but from about 100 yards distance.

These clays first appear as two tiny specs in the distance and at that stage are actually out of effective shot range. They climb upwards and towards you until they are about 25 yards ahead of you. Now, very much like the Springing Teal target they appear to hang momentarily in mid-air before they start to descend. At the start of their descent they look very slow and suddenly appear to become larger as they get closer. Just as we are thinking what easy targets they are, they lose the momentum of flight, respond to the force of gravity and drop like stones, disappearing behind that mound in front of us. I will suggest three ways of approaching this double and as you would expect there are advantages and disadvantages of each.

The first way is to shoot them out in front as a simple driven pair. There is plenty of time to blot both clays out when they are between 40 and 30 yards away and have not lost the momentum of their climbing flight. They are a long way in front therefore very little movement is needed to push the barrels through the clays. It

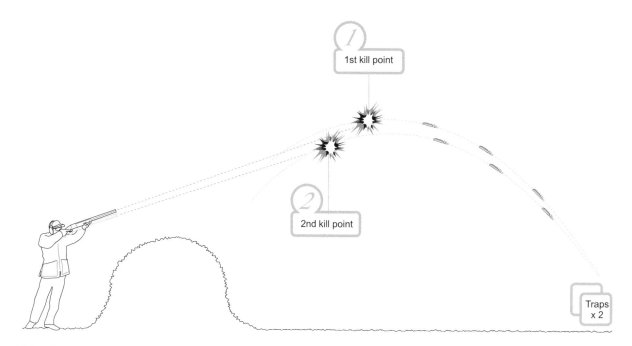

1st kill point

2nd kill point

Traps
x 2

Using The Method to kill Dropping Clays

sounds very simple, and is in reality physically very easy. The flaws in this system are those psychological factors again. The clays look so tiny when you first pick them up that it is hard to convince yourself that they are within effective killing distance, the obvious temptation is to wait until the clays look bigger (easier). However, as you have mentally rehearsed blotting them out, you end up blotting

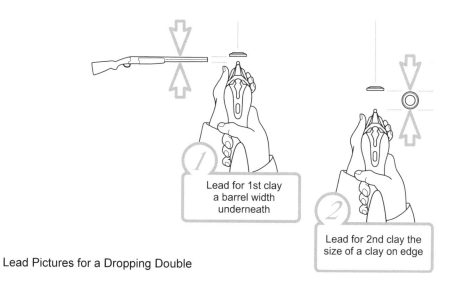

Lead for 1st clay
a barrel width
underneath

Lead for 2nd clay the
size of a clay on edge

Lead Pictures for a Dropping Double

out targets that have now started to descend, consequently shooting well above them.

Let us look at the opposite approach next, which is to maintain the gun down position until the very last minute. The left hand just keeps the bead on the lower of the two clays until it starts to turn on edge to drop with gravity.

The gun is then quickly mounted, pointed and shot beneath the clays. The advantages and disadvantages are the reverse of the 'out in front' approach. Psychologically, the clays appear to look easiest because they are seen to be close and appear comfortably large. The physical realities are that the clays are dropping very fast and that it is very difficult to point the gun far enough below them. Also, the targets are so close (about ten yards) that the shot pattern is still quite tight and therefore less likely to connect with the clay.

The final approach is a middle approach, somewhere between the other two. You are trying to kill the clays just after they have reached their zenith but while they still have some forward flight momentum (before they actually start to drop too quickly). Do not mount the gun too soon or you will result in aiming it. Take the first clay by shooting just underneath it – a kill picture that has a barrel width of daylight between the bottom edge of the clay and the bead. Don't try to be precise about the lead picture, just mount and squeeze the trigger, then point the barrels under the other clay and fire the second shot. The lead or kill picture must be bigger as the second bird is now dropping faster – make it about three barrel widths.

Shoot some of these dropping clays, and try the different approaches to see which you prefer. See if you can make yourself blot them out well in front first. You have killed a couple of them that way, but it takes a lot of conviction doesn't it?

Try the other ways. The temptation to wait until they are very close is hard to resist as you have just discovered. Timing is all important and it requires strong discipline to get it exactly the same for every clay. Don't measure your success and progress on these last doubles. I just wanted you to get the experience of shooting some and to offer some suggestions for coping with them.

The Looper

One more target to finish your lesson on. 'The Looper'. It would be rare to attend any Sporting Clay shoot that did not have at least one looping target.

This clay does as its name suggests. It loops in the air. It might loop left to right, or right to left, or either of those directions, and quartering toward you or away from you.

Your looping target will be flying left to right crossing at 90° about 20 yards in front of you.

Just watch a few of these looping clays in flight. You will note that this particular target moves in three dimensions: It climbs, it crosses and it drops, and therefore causes many clay shots problems. It need not.

I am going to show you a very simple approach to mastering this target. This simple system does however require you to deviate from the Method. You will not be pointing at and moving with this target.

Firstly, you decide on your kill point, which on this target ideally will be about two thirds of the way along its flight path. Any sooner than that will cause you to rush. Much later than that will have the clay dropping very fast.

Now, decide the kill picture. Yes, it is a two dimensional kill picture because the clay is both crossing and dropping.

Visualise a picture that has the barrels about a foot in front of the clay and six inches below it.

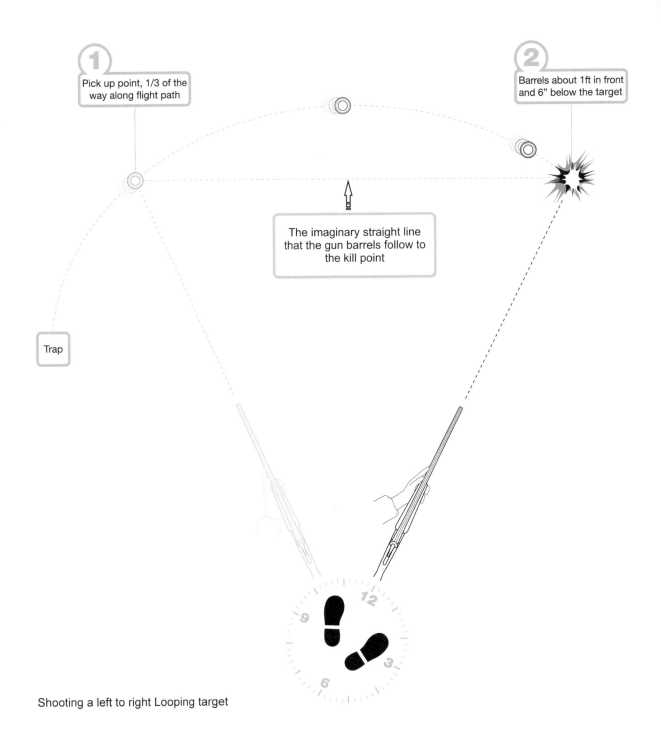

1 Pick up point, 1/3 of the way along flight path

2 Barrels about 1ft in front and 6" below the target

The imaginary straight line that the gun barrels follow to the kill point

Trap

Shooting a left to right Looping target

The last part of the system is to remove the loop. Watch another clay in flight and mentally draw yourself a straight line to the point where the gun barrels will have made the kill picture. Your imaginary straight line for this particular target needs to start about a third of the way along its flight path. Of course, the start point varies with different angled looping targets, but is commonly between a third and halfway along the flight path.

Okay. Try one. No, you are behind the clay and way too high. Yes, the two dimensional kill picture is strange but it is necessary.

Try again. No, your shot is still above the target. Also, you need to remember to lock the stock extra tightly into your cheek, as you are shooting a target moving left to right.

Before calling 'pull', visualise that imaginary straight line and mentally rehearse that kill picture of a foot in front and six inches below the clay.

Take your barrels to a start point a little further along the flight path. Okay. Focus and try again. Well done, a clean kill. That will do for today, you need a rest.

During your next lesson, you can apply your new skills to some typical sporting clay target combinations.

Lesson Six
Pair Combinations

This lesson will enable you to experience the challenges and pleasures of shooting some combinations of sporting clays as doubles. The permutations are of course endless, as the variety of targets is simply decided by the imagination of the person designing the sporting clay layout.

The Going Away and Driven targets 'On Report'

Look at the first pair of clays that you are going to shoot. The first clay flies straight away from you, very similar to the one you learned to shoot during your fourth lesson.

The second (on report) target is a clay driven directly towards you just like the one you shot in your first lesson.

Most important is your preparation deciding the logical sequence of kill point, feet, pick up point, lead picture and gun ready position.

The first clay will need to be shot quickly and instinctively. Your feet will face the trap. You will pick it up a few feet above the trap where you can see it clearly. The kill picture will be the clay sat just above the bead and, as this is a going away target, you will start with the gun mounted.

Now the preparation for the on report target, which is a driven clay. You will be killing it in front of you at about 70° - 80° so there is no need to move your feet. You will need to raise your barrels to point just above the trees in front of you to ensure a good, clear pick up point. Your kill picture will be blotting out the clay by covering it with the barrels, and finally you will be dismounting the gun after the first shot to a relaxed gun down position with the stock about half way up your torso.

Right. Load two cartridges, set yourself up, focus on what you have just mentally rehearsed and call for your first pair of clays.

Kill lost! Try again. Kill lost! Let me make you aware of what is happening here. This is a typical sporting clay situation where the two targets are 'opposites'. By that, I mean that the first clay must be kept in your vision sat just above the bead. However, it is immediately followed by a target that must not be in your vision as you have to blot it out. That simple fact is the cause of your misses, so try again and this time be determined to blot out the 'on report' driven target.

Off you go. Well done, pair killed! Shoot a few more pairs. Focussing on these two different clays as two separate targets makes it much easier, doesn't it?

Let us look at another combination.

Quartering targets 'On Report'

The first target is thrown from a trap behind you, passes you and flies away, but slightly to your right. This target therefore has two dimensions because it is flying away from you but also has some left to right movement. This is commonly called the Quartering Target and needs careful reading.

Now, to the second clay – the 'on report' target. A trap behind you out to your right is throwing a looping clay. However, this is also a quartering target because it is flying away and has some right to left crossing movement.

You have not shot quartering targets before, but you have shot going away and crossing clays, so you will need to combine the two movements.

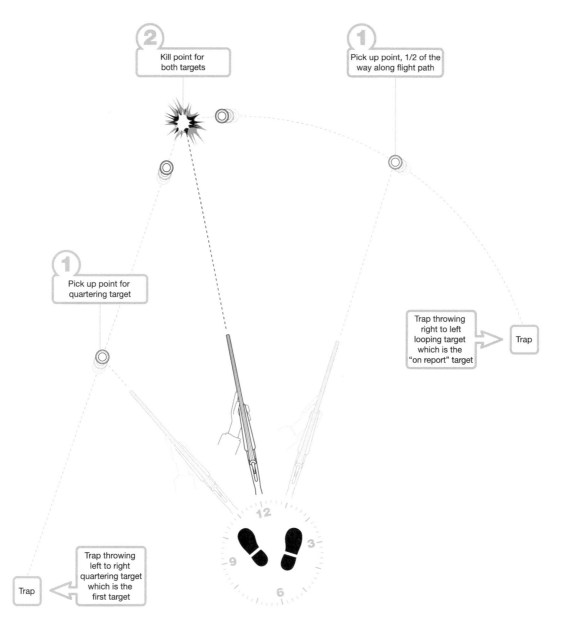

Shooting a left to right Quartering target, followed by a Quartering right to left Looping target as an 'On Report' pair

Because it is flying away you will need to shoot it quickly and instinctively. Any type of going away target requires an 'attacking' attitude. This target also requires a small amount of lead. Mentally visualise a lead picture that has the bead just under and about a standard size clay to the right of the target.

Your pick up point will be critical here, as it is for all fast targets. If you start too far back along the flight path you will chase the target and probably 'flash' past it. Pick it up too late and you are likely to be shooting the target when it is running out of steam and starting to drop.

Watch a few of these quartering clays and carefully decide your pick up point. Remember, you are trying to set up your best reactive situation.

Be careful to set your feet to face your chosen kill point, and finally I suggest you shoot this fast target with a pre-mounted gun.

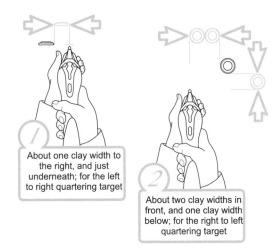

About one clay width to the right, and just underneath; for the left to right quartering target

About two clay widths in front, and one clay width below; for the right to left quartering target

Lead Pictures for these On Report Quartering targets

A tip on picking up fast targets with a pre-mounted gun. Point the gun at the pick up point with the stock locked tight into the cheek and shoulder. Next, lift the head slightly off the stock prior to calling 'pull'. This will improve your field of vision and therefore speed up your reactions. As you lock your gun onto the target, lock your head back onto the stock.

Try a few as singles before you tackle the double. Call when you are ready. You missed above that one. Remember to lock your head back onto the stock as you pick up the target. Try another. Your shot was just left of the target. See a gap the width of a clay to the right of the target. Shoot quickly, approach it aggressively, attack it!

That's better, you are shooting much more quickly.

Now to the looper. Your best kill point is actually about where you were killing that first clay, so no need to move your feet. Remember that straight imaginary line. I would start that line about half way along this looper's flight path. Now the kill picture. Two clays widths in front and one clay width underneath. It is quick, it is quartering away so keep the gun mounted having shot the first clay. The most critical part of your preparation here is to move the barrels very quickly onto your second pick up point (the start of that imaginary line).

Mentally rehearse. Two different kill pictures and two different pick up points. Focus and call when you are ready. Pair killed, well done, well rehearsed.

Take a breather while I show you one more pair of targets.

Simultaneous Crossing pairs

Your final targets for this session are a simultaneous pair of left to right crossing clays. Just to keep it even more interesting, one of the traps is throwing a standard clay and the other is loaded with midi clays.

Watch a pair in flight; there they go, crossing about 25 yards in front of you. Note that the midi clay is about a yard in front of the standard clay, because being smaller and lighter it leaves the trap at greater speed than the standard. The midi clay also looks further away, but don't be fooled. It looks further away simply because it is smaller.

Right then, time for your preparation. Which target are you going to shoot first? Remember your theory: The standard clay being the rear target should be taken first as these clays are flying left to right, and the 'push' in front of the rear clay will naturally move the gun towards the front clay.

Ideally kill the first target when it is straight in front of you. Remember it is left to right and crossing you at 90°, so you have a maximum crossing rate situation. Plenty of lead. Visualise a lead picture that looks like missing two feet in front. You should be trying to kill the second target as soon as you can. Don't let it get too far away from you. Set your feet round to where you will be shooting the second clay so that your torso wants to keep moving in that direction. Finally, do

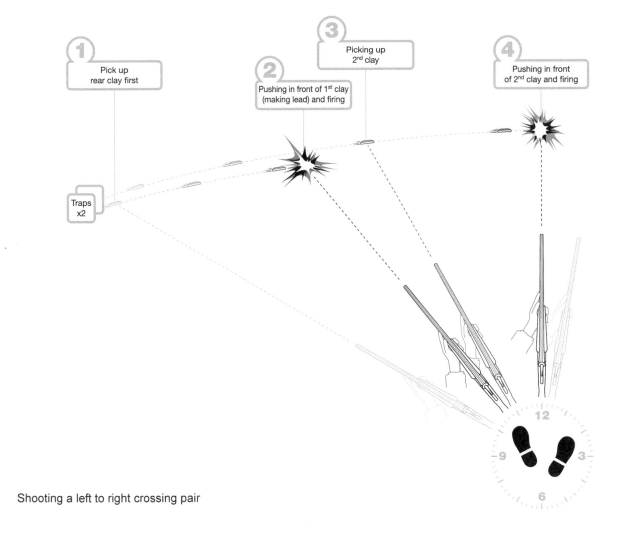

1 Pick up rear clay first

2 Pushing in front of 1st clay (making lead) and firing

3 Picking up 2nd clay

4 Pushing in front of 2nd clay and firing

Traps x2

Shooting a left to right crossing pair

remember to lock the gun extra tightly into your cheek and shoulder. Set yourself up, mentally rehearse those kill pictures. See the barrels two feet in front of both those clays when you are squeezing the trigger. Focus. Call 'pull'. Pair lost. Try again. Pair lost.

Don't worry about the misses. You just have to see more lead. Shoot to miss two feet in front. Take another pair. Pair lost. Don't be frustrated. We will look at another way of shooting this particular pair of targets.

You remember when you first tried simultaneous pairs? Trying to concentrate on one moving target whilst you were optically aware of another was distracting. I think the problem here is that when you are trying to push your barrels two feet in front of the rear clay, your gun is almost pointing at the front clay, which is distracting and confusing you.

Now we will try working to a new plan. The 'Method' is flexible and if one approach is not working it is always a good idea to try another. Set yourself up, same feet positions as before but on this pair pick up the front clay, the midi, and shoot that one first. My theory is that as it is the first one you see you will be on it quickly and able to shoot it just before it is passing 90° in front of you. Also having killed it you will have removed the distraction.

Call for a pair. Kill lost. Great. You powdered that midi clay and only missed the second target because you pushed the stock off your cheek. Reminder – right handers must lock extra tight on left to right crossing targets.

Call again. Fantastic! Pair killed. And again, pair killed. That is great, you deserve your success. Also, a simple example of how there can be more than one way to shoot a target.

As you have discovered, the Method cannot be used completely for all angled targets, but will provide you with a system that you can use to stack the odds in your favour. You are much more likely to be successful with one system that is adaptable to different targets, rather than trying to learn a multitude of different systems to cope with an unknown variety of situations.

To improve your shooting skills, you simply need to practice on a regular basis, at least a couple of times a month would be ideal, with an occasional lesson to sort out any problem targets that you might encounter.

That is enough for this session. We will have a cup of tea in the clubhouse whilst I talk you through some other clay shooting disciplines.

Other Clay Shooting Disciplines

There are three basic types or disciplines of clay pigeon shooting: Sporting, Trap and Skeet.

All have their historic foundations in practice for 'live' bird shooting, though little thought is given nowadays to the origins as all three 'disciplines' have become firmly established as individual competitive clay shooting sports and leisure pursuits.

Sporting, Trap and Skeet are now the recognised titles describing three very different forms of clay shooting. All three encompass a number of different approaches, each having their own specific rules.

Sporting Clays

During your lessons you have been shooting sporting clays. If you were shooting those types of targets in a competition, you would be shooting under the rules of English Sporting Clays, or for overseas readers, just 'Sporting Clays'.

As the rulebook name implies, English Sporting is a clay discipline that started in Britain. However, sporting clay shooting is now the most popular form of clay shooting throughout the world. Its popularity seems to be the limitless variety of targets, and its adaptability to all levels of shooting competence.

At the top level of competition, sporting targets are of course extremely testing, but one or two traps carefully positioned will provide endless hours of pleasure for novice and experienced shots alike.

Corporate Clay shooting

During the last few years, the sudden increase of participation in 'Company Clay Days' has aroused a massive growth of interest in sporting clay shooting. These Company Days have been the 'first' introduction to clay shooting for thousands of people, many of whom subsequently take up the sport as a new found leisure pursuit. A large percentage of these newcomers have no interest in competitive shooting: They are content with the individual and 'private' competition offered by the clay target, and are pleased to enjoy the company of other leisure shooters.

The Sporting discipline is chosen for these events as it is almost certainly the most sociable of all the disciplines.

Flushes and Flurries

In the future you may find yourself enjoying Sporting 'team' events. These are normally Flushes, or the very similar Flurries.

The 'Flush' describes a situation where two or more traps are sited together to throw a number of clays over a team of two, three or four shooters, either in a pre-determined or random sequence.

Flurries present similar pleasures and challenges offered by Flushes, the only difference being in the siting of the traps, which can be two or more presenting targets from different distances and directions.

These team Flushes are very popular at charity fund raising events and corporate clay days.

There are no formal rules as competitions are fairly relaxed affairs governed by local rules. Safety is of course as always of paramount importance, so Flushes are shot with individual team members shooting from within shooting safety cages which prevent barrels from being pointed towards danger arcs.

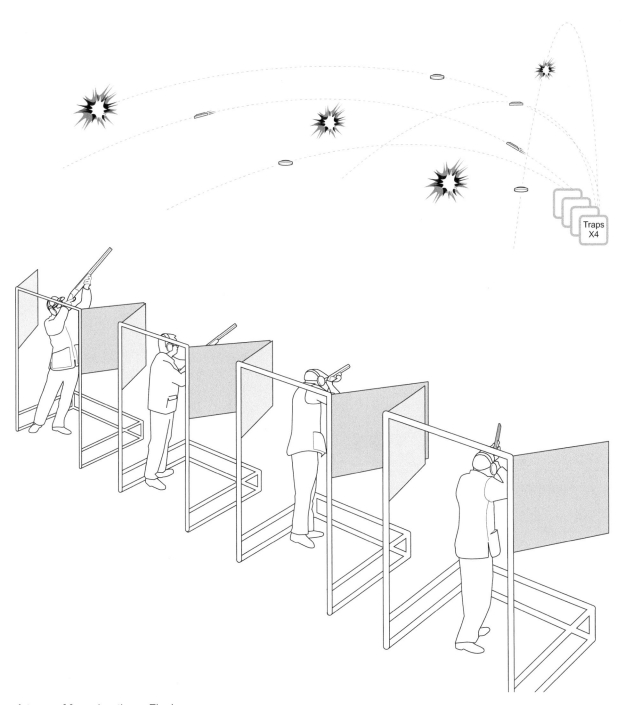

Traps
X4

A team of four shooting a Flush

There is a special fascination and excitement for both participants and spectators at team flushes! Once the Flush has been activated by the initial 'pull' or 'ready' any predictability has vanished. Consider that a four man team will often be confronted by six clays in the air at any one time. Those six clays might also be of different sizes, colours, heights, speeds and angles! It is the coolest and most

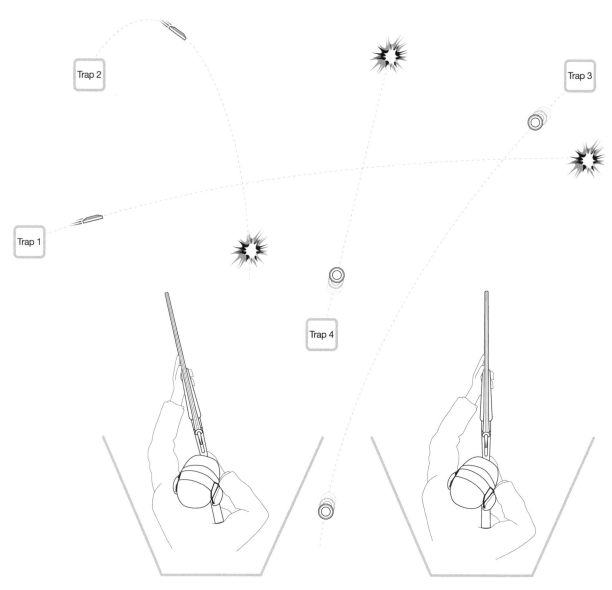

A team of two shooting a Flurry with four traps

disciplined teams that win Flushes. Most flush targets are 'lost' by team members getting flustered and being caught unloaded rather than inaccurate shooting.

The theory of successful Team Flush shooting is to devise a plan of who will shoot which targets. Once the flush has started each team member must have implicit trust in his partners whilst trying to discipline himself to stick to his part of the shooting plan. All bodes well until the first 'lost' target. It requires tremendous discipline to let a miss go if your gun is loaded. If you kill it, you'll soon have a pair of clays over your head. But both your barrels are empty! Another team member kills your pair, he is then caught unloaded! Result – chaos and curses, but tremendous fun.

I have been both witness and participant to some wonderful and sophisticated pre-Flush shoot plans. Only rarely do these come to fruition! On these occasions the pleasure of the spectators equals the satisfaction of the participants.

FITASC
The latest and probably toughest addition to our Sporting disciplines is FITASC.

This most challenging form of sporting shooting is the French version of practice for field shooting. It was formalised by them as a regulated competitive clay discipline in the 1960s and has become immensely popular and fiercely contested worldwide. Its French title 'Parcours de chasse' roughly translates as claybird shooting 'Sporting'. In other parts of the world it is often called 'International Sporting' but most British shooters know it by the abbreviated letters of the governing body, 'Federation Internationale de Tir Aux Armes Sportive de Chasse' (FITASC).

When you start to practice on the sporting layouts here you will normally shoot over five stands (shooting positions) with five pairs of targets at each stand (so you get to improve your scores by having repeat pairs of the same targets).

The prime difference and therefore increased challenge is that on a FITASC layout you only get to shoot each target or pair of targets once!

There is also a mandatory gun ready position which the rules specify as 'gun held with two hands clearly out of the shoulder. Gun touching the body under the armpit'. The competitor is not allowed to move from this gun ready position until the target or targets appear into view.

One hundred targets is usually the minimum for FITASC competition, though 150 to 200 is common. Most FITASC competitions are of at least one full day's duration, with the bigger competitions often being staged over two, three, four or even five days, depending on the number of entrants.

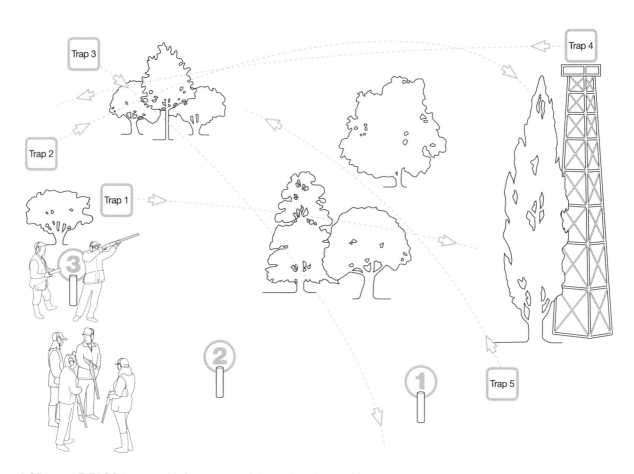

A 25 target FITASC layout, with five traps and three shooting positions

You don't stroll into a FITASC shoot and wander around the stands deciding which one to shoot first! Competitors are separated into squads of up to six and are given their order of layouts to shoot in strict rotation. Each layout consists of 25 targets, offering a varied sequence of singles and doubles. At each layout the competitors shoot a number of targets from different shooting positions or 'posts'. Each member of the squad takes a turn to be the first to shoot at each post as the sequence is shown and explained only once. No competitor is allowed to watch other squads in action at other stands. The complete range of Standard, Midi, Mini and blaze (coloured) clays are used, plus Rabbit and Battue clays. Targets tend to be at longer ranges than in English Sporting, with the added challenge of a great variation of speeds, angles, distances, combinations and so on.

FITASC is certainly not for the feint hearted, and is only really suitable to those who are already experienced and successful in English Sporting. It is a great credit to our top sporting shooters that they have achieved gold medals in all classes during World Championships.

The 'Trap' Disciplines

The Trap Disciplines are distinct from Sporting Disciplines, in that the target is always going away from you, you always call Pull from the gun pre-mounted position, shooting takes place in squads, and it tends to be less sociable.

DTL - a brief history

The oldest and most basic form of Trap shooting is 'Down the Line', commonly known by the abbreviated DTL title. The first DTL championships were held in 1893, and as a shooting discipline is a direct descendant of practice and competition shooting of 'live' birds.

Many of the landed gentry of the 19th century were avid enthusiasts of the various forms of Game Shooting. Their feathered quarry was generally shot as going away targets, having been flushed from cover by servants and dogs.

Live birds released from traps, Notting Hill Gun Club circa 1880s

Regardless of wealth, privilege and the abundance of 'Game Birds' it was not practicable for the Gentry to shoot year round. In order to maintain their shooting practice a group of enthusiasts decided that pigeons, starlings, sparrows and so on could provide a substitute. Servants were despatched to net or otherwise capture these birds. When sufficient live targets were captured they were returned to the assembled group of waiting Gentry. A servant was allocated to each of the gentlemen, who would remove their 'top hats'. The servants were instructed to place each top hat on the ground a set distance in front of the gentlemen, and a pigeon would then be 'trapped' under each hat. The unfortunate bird would have had the tail feathers removed, since without tail feathers it flies erratically and provides an unpredictable target! Strings were attached to the top hats, and led back to the shooting positions. Each gentleman would take his turn at shooting at a pigeon as it was freed from its trap under the hat, when the servant was instructed to 'pull' the string.

This form of shooting became very popular and a mechanical trap device soon replaced the top hat. It was not long before competitive rules were established and the informed groups of gentry became formalised into teams or 'squads' of six. Competition was fierce and great sums of money were won and lost.

Although this barbaric sport was not banned by legislation until 1921, it soon was the focus for much public pressure. Various mechanical devices that would throw suitable inanimate targets were manufactured. Naturally, they were called 'traps'. Glass bulbs (some filled with feathers) were popular targets for a while, until the first 'clay pigeon' targets were introduced from the USA during the early 1920s - originally made from baked clay, but soon changed to the more reliable substance of mixed pitch and lime.

DTL today

Other than the increased sophistication in traps, guns and cartridges, the modern DTL shoot is little changed from those of the 1890s.

Squads of six shooters move 'down the line' of five shooting positions or stations, situated 16 yards behind a protected trap position sunk into the ground. About 2 ½ feet of the trap house is all that is visible to the shooting squad. Each squad member calls 'pull' for his single target from each shooting station. Only standard size clays are used, but they may be coloured white or orange if thrown against dark backgrounds.

The trap must be capable of throwing the clay at least 50 yards on a set trajectory in calm air. It must also be able to oscillate randomly across an angle of 45°.

Gun calibre and cartridge rules are the same as English sporting. Most serious trap shooters however will be opting for No. 7 or No. 7 ½ shot and using 'Trap Guns'. Their guns will generally have longer barrels – 30" or even 32" – and be heavier than most sporting guns. Most trap guns are set up to 'shoot high',

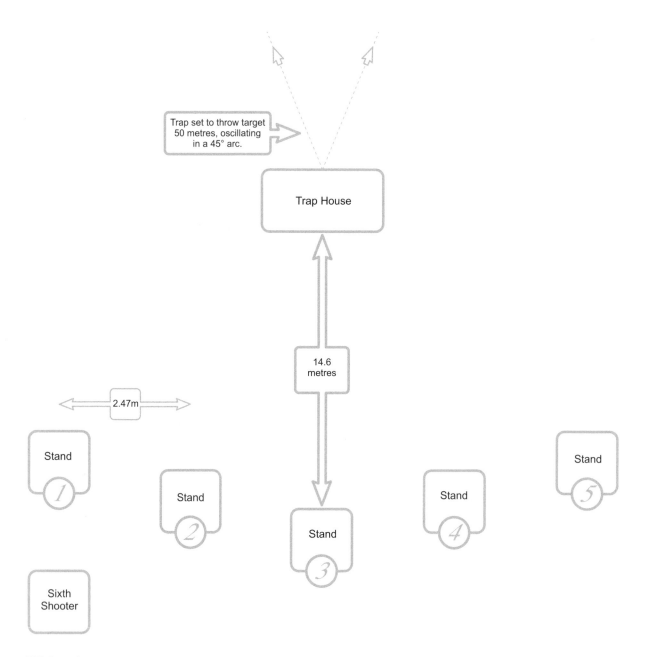

Trap set to throw target 50 metres, oscillating in a 45° arc.

Trap House

14.6 metres

2.47m

Stand

1

Stand

2

Stand

3

Stand

4

Stand

5

Sixth Shooter

DTL layout

enabling the shooter to point well underneath the clay target, thereby achieving a clearer 'sight picture'.

DTL has a loyal following of enthusiasts, but nothing like the numbers enjoying sporting clays, probably because it is not so sociable and lacks the variety of the target mix.

The longer barrels and increased weight are considered more suitable for a steady point on a going away target that has little relative crossing movement. That extra weight will also absorb more recoil, which is important when you consider that every squad member will fire at least 25 cartridges on a single round of DTL, and that most competitions are over 100 targets.

When the DTL squad member calls for his first target of the round, he knows he has two shots to kill a single clay. If he kills with the first barrel, he will score three points, the second barrel, two points. He knows that there are 24 more targets in that round which will be thrown at unknown random angles within 45°. He is acutely aware that too many second barrel kills will leave him out of the placings, and that there are three more rounds to follow.

The shooter adopts the pre-mounted gun ready position; gun position is optional, but there is no time for gun mounting in trap shooting. His success will depend on his ability to maintain total concentration on his precise style of shooting. This necessary attitude leaves little room for social discourse!

Double Rise, Single Barrel, and Handicap By Distance

There are three variations to the DTL discipline, though none of them have a massive following. They all utilise the same layout and equipment and are simply variations on a theme.

'Double Rise' is merely DTL but with the traps throwing a simultaneous double at a pre-set angle within the defined area of DTL targets. Competitors may only fire one barrel at each target of the pair, scoring five points for a pair killed and two points for one kill. 'Single Barrel' follows the same format as DTL, the only difference being that only one shot is allowed at each target.

'Handicap by Distance' is a DTL competition between shooters of varying classes. The top class squad members are 'handicapped' by moving back from the trap house, up to distances of 23 yards.

ABT, UT and OT (Olympic Trap)

There are three other Trap disciplines all based on the going away target and shooting squads principles of DTL. In a logical order of sophistication and challenge, first on the list is ABT or Automatic Ball Trap, where the layout is very similar to DTL.

Squads of six shooters rotate through five stations placed along a 15 metre radius line, which is marked out to the rear of the trap house. The ABT trap house is sunk into the ground, with its top flush with the ground and level with the surface of the shooting station. The trap must be capable of throwing a standard size clay up to 80 metres in still air. It is required to swing at random within a 90° range, enabling the target to be thrown in an unpredictable direction up to 45° either side of the centre line. Additionally, the trap must be able to randomly elevate and depress at the same time, so that when the clay has travelled 10 metres from the trap house its height will be between one and four metres.

Squad members may take two shots at each target. They score one point for a kill regardless of firing one or two shots.

The rules for gun and cartridge use are the same as DTL. The extra challenges obviously relate to the speed of the target, which is travelling faster than a DTL target because it is set up to throw further. The shooter is further tested as the target will be projected through random directions within the 90° arc, and at varying heights.

ABT is next in popularity with trap shooters to DTL, but is seen as a much tougher discipline by many DTL enthusiasts. This is probably why it attracts a smaller

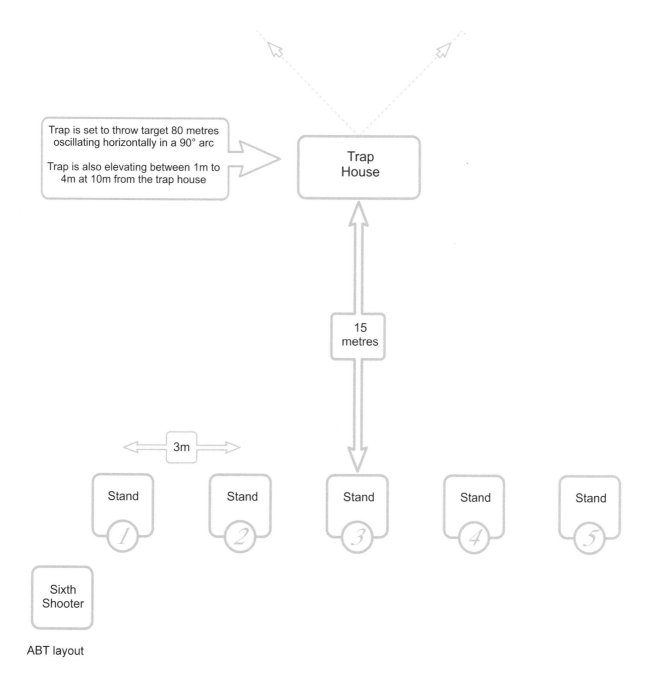

Trap is set to throw target 80 metres oscillating horizontally in a 90° arc

Trap is also elevating between 1m to 4m at 10m from the trap house

Trap House

15 metres

3m

Stand

1

Stand

2

Stand

3

Stand

4

Stand

5

Sixth Shooter

ABT layout

following. It is immensely popular on the continent and is in fact governed by International Shooting rules, as are the remaining two trap disciplines.

Universal Trench (UT) is very similar to ABT in the speeds, distances, heights and angles of the targets. A squad of six take turns at shooting from five stations set in

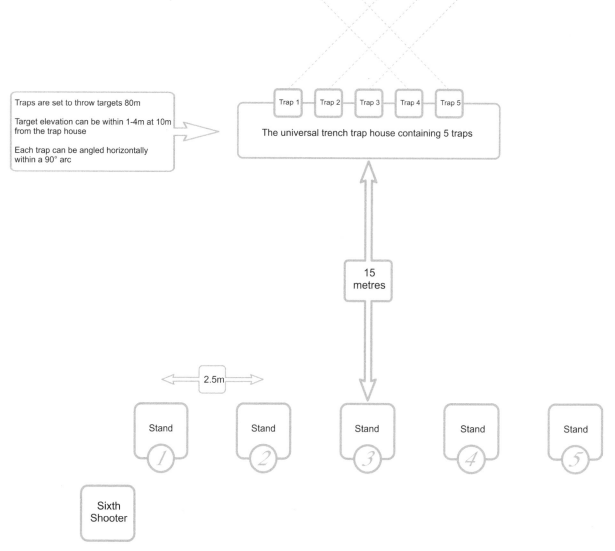

Traps are set to throw targets 80m

Target elevation can be within 1-4m at 10m from the trap house

Each trap can be angled horizontally within a 90° arc

Trap 1 — Trap 2 — Trap 3 — Trap 4 — Trap 5

The universal trench trap house containing 5 traps

15 metres

2.5m

Stand *1*

Stand *2*

Stand *3*

Stand *4*

Stand *5*

Sixth Shooter

UT layout

a straight line 15 metres behind the trap house. The prime difference is that there are five traps not one. Each squad member is allowed two shots at one target from each station, scoring one point for a kill. The target may be thrown from any one of the five traps. After each five targets of a round, the traps are re-adjusted to throw clays at different angles and heights. There are pre-determined trap positions for each round of 25 targets to ensure that all members of the squad are presented with the same number of height and angle variations. The pre-determined trap position sequences are not known to the squad. UT has a very small following in Britain, though it is extremely popular in Europe.

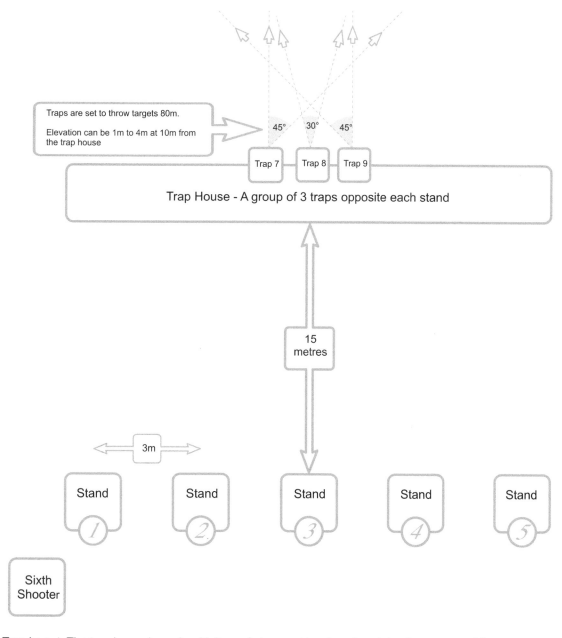

Traps are set to throw targets 80m.

Elevation can be 1m to 4m at 10m from the trap house

45°   30°   45°

Trap 7   Trap 8   Trap 9

Trap House - A group of 3 traps opposite each stand

15 metres

3m

Stand 1   Stand 2   Stand 3   Stand 4   Stand 5

Sixth Shooter

Olympic Trap layout. The trap house is sunk, with its roof at ground level, and contains five groups of three traps

The ultimate in challenge and sophistication in Trap shooting is 'Olympic Trap' (OT or Trench). As the title implies, it is one of only three clay disciplines staged as an Olympic Games competition. The trap house for OT is a large trench containing fifteen automatic traps set in five banks of three.

Five stations are spaced in line 15 metres directly behind each of the five triple trap positions.

Standard clays of colours suitable to the background are thrown at similar speeds and trajectories as ABT and UT.

OT squads follow the same single target from each station routine. On the call of 'pull' the clay is thrown from one of the three traps directly in front of the shooter.

Two shots may be used for each target, with one point being awarded for a kill. Pre-determined sequences similar to Universal Trap are used. Trap release sequence, angles and height are changed after every 50 targets during competitions, which are normally of at least 100 targets.

Britain has a keen (if not frustrated) group of OT enthusiasts. Our OT shooters have problems in gaining sufficient practice owing to the lack of facilities. Very few shooting grounds can afford the huge financial outlay of 15 automatic traps per layout.

'Double Trap' is the most modern of all clay shooting disciplines. It joined Olympic Skeet and Olympic Trap as the third Clay Shooting event during the 1996 Atlanta Olympic Games.

Double trap events are shot on a standard Olympic trap layout. Squads of six each shoot 25 pairs of clays thrown from two of the three traps in the centre bank. The

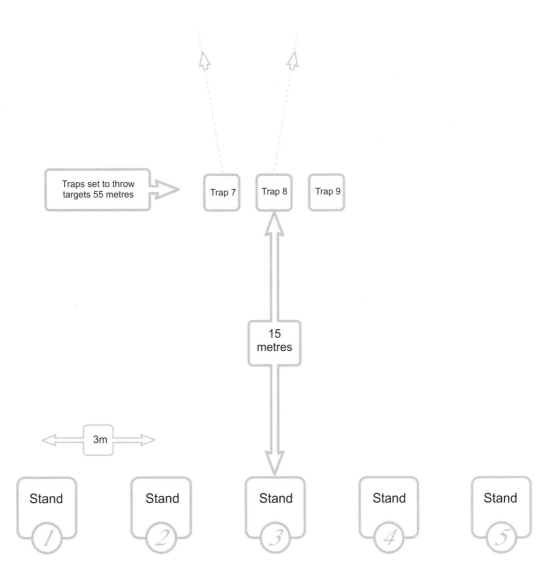

Traps set to throw targets 55 metres

Trap 7   Trap 8   Trap 9

15 metres

3m

Stand 1   Stand 2   Stand 3   Stand 4   Stand 5

Double Trap layout

clays are thrown left, straight or right in 'set schemes'. The traps must be capable of throwing standard sized clays 55 metres in still air.

Skeet (Round the Clock)

Skeet, the third main discipline had its origins in the USA. Whilst our landed gentry were practising their game shooting at 'live' pigeon events, American farmers were devising practice facilities for their own style of field (quail) shooting. Legend has it that one such enthusiast had been given the idea of clay targets having watched youths skimming clam shells across a lake.

Meanwhile a keen field shooting farmer had hit upon the idea of a simple practice facility by siting a clay target trap on the perimeter of a large circle. His simple theory was that by throwing a clay target on one trajectory and shooting from various positions right around the circle, every conceivable angle of shot could be practised.

This 'Round the Clock' shooting soon became popular, and quite quickly competitions were being staged. As it rapidly popularised its major drawback was evident – the impossibility of maintaining safety areas, when shooting through 360 degrees. The solution was as obvious as the attraction of the original 'Round the Clock' idea: Place a trap directly opposite the first one and shoot from positions along the perimeter of a semi-circle between the two. This 'half clock' system was taken up by an enthusiastic following across the USA around which localised competitions were staged.

An arms company sponsored a competition via the National press, the winner being the person who forwarded the most appropriate name for this new sport. 'Skeet' (a Scandinavian interpretation of Shoot) was the winning nomination.

In Britain we mainly stage our own version (English Skeet) but also have a small following of the other two – 'American' and ISU (International Shooting Union). The latter is the other clay shooting discipline staged at Olympic Games.

All three Skeet disciplines operate around the same basic layout which consists of 'high' and 'low' trap houses sited 42 yards apart.

The high house trap throws a single standard size clay from a height of about 10-feet above ground level. The trap is adjusted to throw the target about 55 yards and pass about six yards to the left of the mid-point of the trap houses. At this point the target should be about 15 feet high; the low house trap throws its clay from 3½ feet above ground level. This clay should pass six yards to the right of the midway point at a similar height and speed to the high house target.

A round of 'English Skeet' consists of 25 targets in a set sequence of singles and simultaneous doubles. Squads of shooters take their turns from seven shooting stations evenly spaced along a semi-circular arc having a radius of about 15 yards from the midway point.

Each squad member takes two singles and two doubles from stations 1, 2, 4, 6 and 7, and two singles from stations 3 and 5. He is allowed one shot at each target scoring one point for a kill. From stations 1 and 2 the high house target of doubles must be shot at first. At 6 and 7 the same rules apply to the low house target. At station 4, the shooter nominates which target of the double he will shoot first.

The sequence of singles and doubles makes up 24 targets. The 25th target is taken after the first target missed, or as a choice of a high or low house single taken from station 7 when the shooter has achieved 24 kills.

The gun and cartridge rules are similar to the trap disciplines, though cartridge loads and shot size may not be varied during a round. As targets are fast and close, most Skeet shooters opt for the winder spread of English number 9 or equivalent.

Gun ready position is optional, though most competitors opt for a 'gun down' position and use shorter barrels with open chokes (26" – 28").

The skills are a combination of the 'pure shooting' abilities of sporting and the concentration of trap. To be successful the skeet shooter also requires the ability to retain and achieve a great variety of 'pick up' and 'kill' positions and sight pictures. English Skeet has a keen following of competitive shooters and is also attractive to Sporting shots who appreciate the opportunity to shoot a variety of different angled targets in a short space of time. A competent squad can complete a 25 target round in less than 30 minutes. I'm sure many clay shooters would try their hand and take up Skeet, if there were only more facilities.

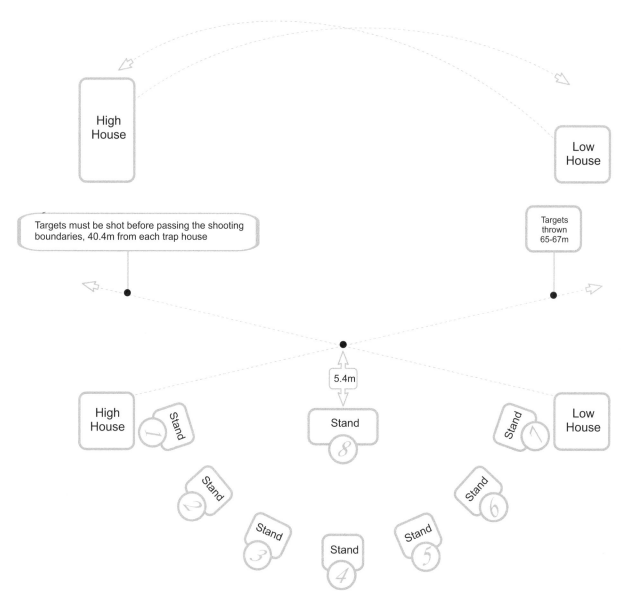

ISU Skeet layout, as used at the Olympics. An English Skeet layout has the same dimensions, but doesn't have the centre station number 8.

ISU is the most testing of the three Skeet disciplines. The layout is the same as English, with the addition of an eighth station at the midway point, where one driven single is taken from each trap house. Targets are faster, being thrown to travel at least 71 yards. To add further challenges, there is a random delay of between 0 to 3 seconds on the call of 'pull', plus a mandatory gun down position specified in the rules as, 'holding the gun with both hands so that the gun butt touches the crest of the hip bone'. A competitor may not move from this gun ready position until the target has appeared.

This style of Skeet shooting mainly attracts the very skilful. Consequently the majority of skeet layouts that are available are set up for 'English', making it difficult for ISU hopefuls to gain practice.

The least common skeet discipline found in Britain is 'American' (they called it NSSA Skeet). As far as I am aware, you will only find it in this country on US forces bases. The layout, target speeds and trajectories are the same as English Skeet, but with the inclusion of an eighth station. The Americans stage one type of 100 target competition where each round of 25 targets is shot with a different calibre: .410, 28 bore, 20 bore and 12 bore!

Helice (ZZ)

There is one other clay shooting discipline that does not fit under the Trap, Skeet, or Sporting umbrella. It is commonly known as ZZ (Zig Zag), but officially called 'Helice'. This event first appeared in the 1960s as a direct descendant of the type of 'live' pigeon shooting still taking place at that time in some parts of the continent. The erratic flight of the Helice target is intended to represent the unpredictable flight path of the 'live' bird minus tail feathers.

It could be argued that 'Helice' (French for helicopter) is not actually a clay shooting discipline. The target, whilst similar in size and shape to a standard clay, is actually a white plastic disc. This disc is clipped into a plastic circle that has two propeller blades protruding from it, like helicopter rotors. They are actually very

reminiscent of the toy helicopters that were popular some years ago – the type that released a plastic circle on the pull of a string.

There are five traps which are little more than electric motors set into the ground, and a target is placed upon the spindle of each. The traps are switched on which causes the target to rotate on the spindle and rock from side to side. On the call of 'pull' a target is released at random, flying erratically upwards and in any direction.

Helice target on its launcher. Also shown are the other four launchers of a Helice layout.

The competitor is allowed two shots at each target, and is required to knock out a visible piece of the white central disc to score a kill. He must achieve this before the target has crossed over a perimeter line, which is a circular fence two feet high, 21 metres from the centre trap.

The shooting position is also 21 metres from the centre trap, although the shooter may be required to move back up to seven metres during a 'handicap' competition.

Helice is the least followed clay discipline in Britain. In fact, I know of only three shooting grounds that are currently staging this event. It is very time consuming and requires the destruction of very expensive targets.

Helice target in flight

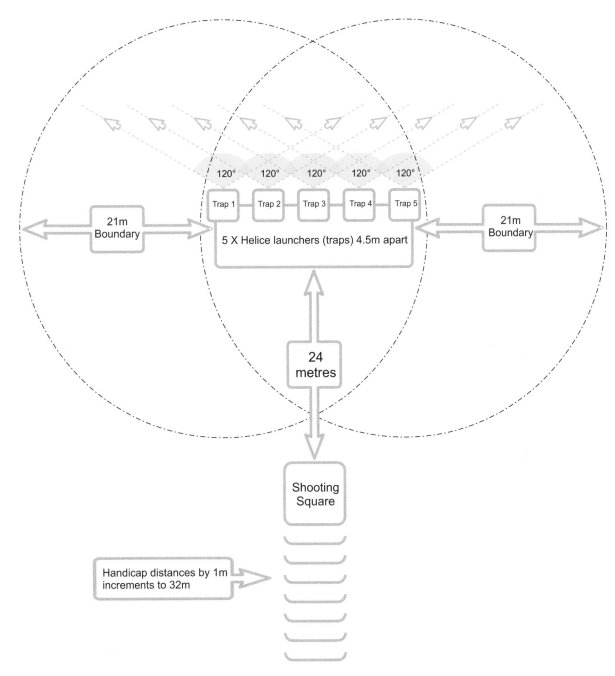

Helice layout

Despite the lack of 'Helice' practice facilities in this country, Britain has its share of gold medal (male and female) winners in international events.

Enjoying Your Clay Shooting

Having completed an introductory course of tuition, you are naturally fired with enthusiasm and keenness to progress. Enjoy your clay shooting, but don't let your enthusiasm cause you unrealistic expectations of your success rate. You will benefit greatly from your lessons, as they have provided you with a solid foundation upon which you can build and steadily improve your shooting skills.

It is important to remember that no amount of lessons within the privacy of the shooting school can substitute for the learning experience (and pleasure) of shooting alongside other clay enthusiasts.

The voice of experience

No doubt you will experience some setbacks and disappointments in the future, but you can minimise them if you heed the simple words of caution and advice that I am going to offer you.

Firstly: Pick one discipline to practice on to begin with. As your lessons have been based on Sporting type targets, it is only logical that you concentrate on that discipline initially. Choose your shooting venues and the company that you shoot in carefully.

Of course you want to improve your scores, but avoid competitive shoots where you are competing against others for a while. Just remember you can enjoy competing against a moving target every time you call 'pull'. Concentrate on your own scores and don't measure your progress and success against other people's scores. If you could kill four out of 10 driven clays six weeks ago, and can now consistently kill seven or eight, you are improving your skills. What others are scoring is of no relevance to your own progress.

Ideally, your fellow shooters should be of a similar standard to yourself. Of course you will learn from watching others. Indeed it is always pleasurable, watching skilful clayshots, and you can and should learn from them. We all learn from copying, but be careful who you try to emulate.

The person you will learn best watching is someone of similar build and physique as yourself, who shoots the same system as yourself. It will be a real bonus if that particular person is prepared to help you, assuming he or she communicates at your level. Clayshots are a friendly crowd and especially generous with their advice. Only you can decide which advice is helpful to you.

Sporting clay shots are probably the friendliest and most sociable of all. By all means enjoy the sociable aspects of Sporting shoots but don't forget those crucial seconds that should be spent on reading the targets.

If you want to shoot the Method consistently well, you must always spend time on your mental preparation. The basic requirement of choosing: **Kill point, feet position, pickup point, lead picture and gun ready position** will always be important.

Most novices that I meet become interested in the various shooting publications. Indeed reading these is surely an extension of the shooting hobby. Every month, clay shooting magazines encourage us to improve our success by changing barrel length, chokes, cartridges and technique. Fashion exists in all walks of life. Currently we are assured that 32" barrels are a must and why should the novice shot be prevented from following 'fashion'?

By all means experiment, but stick with the gun and cartridge combination that you know works within your own limitations until you have gained more confidence.

Competition

Sooner or later, you may want to enter a competition and if you are that keen, have a go! But make it later rather than sooner. When you enter your first competition follow these simple rules:

1. Get there early and allow yourself time to unwind from travel.

2. Walk around and assess the layout.

3. Choose a stand that has targets that you feel most confident about tackling, and then tackle the other stands in a logical sequence of increasing difficulty.

4. On the stands where the targets look impossible, discipline yourself to plan how you can use the 'Method' to your best advantage. Most stands will be doubles. If necessary, just concentrate on the target that looks marginally easier. Better to give a 100% effort and two barrels on one clay, than half-hearted attempts at two clays.

5. Don't dwell on targets that you have missed, and don't dwell on how many more targets remain to be tackled. Just give 100% concentration on the job in hand every time you call 'pull'.

6. In your early competitive attempts, don't try to compensate for a dismal score by taking a re-entry card. The chances are that you will be so bogged down in your previous score that you will fair even more poorly. Your time will be better spent watching those who are shooting well. You will also be reassured by seeing others far more experienced than yourself missing plenty of clays.

Only you can decide if you enjoy competitive clay shooting. Those who win at the top level deserve their successes. Most of them will tell you that they never practice. The reality is that there is only one form of practice for competitive clay shooting, and that is to compete regularly.

Just be reassured that you need never compete against anyone else to fully enjoy your clay shooting. There will always be a private competition between you, the moving clay, and your own last score.

Allowing your skill to develop

You are likely to encounter at some stage a target that you just can't master. The first time it happens walk away, forget it and shoot something that you feel confident about.

If the next time you meet it you suffer the same disastrous results, walk away again. Leave it alone until you can arrange a professional lesson to master that particular target. If you don't the chances are that this target will become your 'bogey'.

When you are comfortable with your Sporting shooting, try another discipline. Keep your early scores in perspective, just remind yourself how much work you put into building your Sporting scores. It is unlikely that you will become equally good at more than one discipline. Concentrate on the one that you enjoy most, and be satisfied with a reasonable level of competence at any other.

Forget the losses. Remember the kills, and you too can enjoy a lifetime's pleasure of clay shooting.

Your own gun

There is still no need for you to dash off and buy a gun. The 20 bore that you have been using during your lessons fits you and seems to suit you well, so you are very welcome to borrow it while you are practising.

When you are ready to buy, a similar 20 bore would be an ideal first gun choice at your stage of shooting.

When you do buy one, I will take it to my gunsmith who will alter it to fit you and make it comfortable for you to shoot, just like the one that you have been using. That one has 28 inch fixed choke barrels with the chokes opened right out.

To date you have been using number 7 ½ 24 gram fibre wadded cartridges, which I think is a good 20 bore compromise, but by all means try number 7s or number 8s. Cartridges, just like guns, calibres, chokes and barrel length are subjective matters.

I have simply expressed my opinion about what has been working well for some-one of your physical stature. However, I learned long ago that the advice I give is only followed for a short period. Sooner or later (and it is generally sooner!) the novice shot will be influenced by family, friends, magazines, books, DVDs and gun shop staff on the merits of the latest and most 'fantastic' new cartridges. Also, of course, it's perfectly normal that you will wish to experiment.

I am very confident that a 20 bore altered to a proper fit will provide you with comfortable, enjoyable shooting. However, when you gain more experience and confidence as you shoot more regularly at different venues, it is highly likely that you will move up to a 12 bore.

The 12 bore over and under, with a variety of changeable screw in chokes (multi chokes) is by far the most popular choice among regular clay shots.

When you do have your own gun that has been fitted for you, I will be encourag-ing you to practice gun mounting in front of a mirror. Now let me explain how you practice.

Take the gun, load it with snap caps and stand about six feet away from a mirror that is big enough to reflect at least the top half of your body. You must obviously advise everybody else within the house what you are about to do so that you do not cause alarm. Also, I would suggest that you do not do this exercise when chil-dren are present as they might get the impression that guns are things which are 'played' with in the house!

Stand comfortably in front of the mirror and take up the gun ready position, choosing the reflection of your right eye as the pick up point. Now slowly and deliberately mount the gun, making sure your left hand keeps the bead level with the pick up point.

You will notice immediately if your right hand is taking over, as you will see the barrels dip below your eye reflection.

When you have the gun fully and correctly mounted, you should just be able to see the top half of your eye reflection above the bead.

Repeat the mounting exercise, speeding up the mount each time. When you are mounting the gun quickly and comfortably, try closing your eyes until the gun is in the shoulder and cheek. If you see the right sight picture above the bead, you have achieved a perfect gun mount.

Try to discipline yourself to this exercise for a couple of minutes two or three times a week. If you do, it will become instinctive for you to point your left hand at the first part of your gun mount. Your body will also instinctively feel a correct gun mount.

Closing thoughts

I hope I have achieved the objectives stated in the introduction.

It has been my intention throughout these chapters to convince all beginners that there is a straightforward and simple route to safe, enjoyable shooting.

I really do hope that I have managed to encourage the 'undecided' newcomers to 'have a go' and that they have a clear idea of a logical course to follow.

Hopefully, experienced shots will be able to use my approach to shooting tuition in their efforts to teach others. To those I would ask that they try to remember how awkward and nervous they felt when they first picked up a shotgun.

Anyone about to teach shotgun shooting for the first time should shoot a few targets from the 'wrong' shoulder. The awkwardness you experience is very akin to how the beginner feels. Be patient with them, and you will be rewarded with immense pleasure in their successes.

John King - the author

John King is one of the country's most experienced and sought after shooting coaches.

He has 55 years of shotgun shooting experience, training some 30,000 people in the enjoyment and safe practice of shooting.

His passion started as a boy of ten, rough shooting in the Warwickshire countryside. He went on to serve in the Royal Navy for 25 years, acting as a trainer in a variety of weaponry.

It was at the Royal Navy Leadership school in Wiltshire in the early 1970s that John had his first encounter with clay targets, and he became totally committed to the sport: As well as coaching Naval personnel during the week he was coaching at weekends in the Wiltshire countryside near his home. He went on to design and open the Royal Navy's first clay shooting venue at Portland in Dorset, and was instrumental in getting clay shooting established as a recognised Royal Navy sport.

John qualified as a C.P.S.A. coach, and became a Senior Sporting Coach in 1984. When he left the Royal Navy in 1987 he opened the now renowned Barbury Shooting School with his wife Maureen. He soon built up an enviable reputation for his unique style of coaching both nationally and internationally; John has designed private clay shooting layouts at home and abroad, and has taken his coaching skills to the U.S.A.

In the late 1980s John put together the first ever coaches course for the B.A.S.C. (British Association for Shooting and Conservation). He has trained many other coaches since then, and their successes are testament to his depth of knowledge. He then began writing articles in shooting magazines and had his first clay shooting book published in 1991.

John's coaching style is relaxed and without frills. He is adamant that coaching should be simple, and should always be fun for the pupils. His pupils would describe their lessons as highly informative enjoyable experiences, and John has skilfully presented this book so that you will have a similar enjoyable experience.

For 10 years John has combined his shooting coaching with Executive Life Coaching, where he has used his considerable leadership and psychology training. He has gained qualifications in Neuro Linguistic Programming (NLP), and now uses the Inner Game NLP techniques adopted by many top level sports psychologists in his shooting coaching - to great effect.

John and Maureen sold Barbury Shooting School in 2007, although John very happily remains there as a much sought after coach.

www.johnkingcoaching.com
admin@johnkingcoaching.com
Swindon, Wiltshire, UK